The Victorian Staffordshire Figure

A Guide for Collectors

1. Frontispiece of *A Representation of the Manufacturing of Earthenware*, published in London, 35, Bury Street St James's, 1827. This and other copper engravings from the same source are by courtesy of Mr Gordon Elliott. The City Museum and Art Gallery, Stoke-on-Trent.

ANTHONY OLIVER

The Victorian
Staffordshire Figure

A Guide for Collectors

HEINEMANN : LONDON

William Heinemann Ltd
15 Queen St, Mayfair, London W1X 8BE
LONDON MELBOURNE TORONTO
JOHANNESBURG AUCKLAND

First published 1971
Reprinted 1972, 1978

© Anthony Oliver 1971
434 54390 X

Unless otherwise stated, all photographs, both black-and-white and colour, are by courtesy of Oliver-Sutton Antiques, 34c Kensington Church Street, London W.8.

Filmset and printed in Great Britain by
BAS Printers Limited, Over Wallop, Hampshire

Contents

No art with Potters can compare
we make our Pots of what we Potters are.
                                   (anonymous Staffordshire potter)

To these unknown potters of Staffordshire
this book is dedicated with affection.

Preface

I bought my first Victorian Staffordshire figure twenty-five years ago and I have been collecting ever since. I hope this book will answer some of the many questions that puzzled me when I tried to find out more about them.

Acknowledgements

My thanks are due to so many people, not only for the help I received when I was writing this book, but also for the countless kindnesses shown me through the years of collecting and research that preceded it.

For a long time I believed that acknowledgements at the beginning of books, like the credits at the beginning of films, were a necessary bore, and to some extent I still believe this to be true. At least I believe it to be true for the average reader or film audience, for those who have not been, so to speak, concerned with the production. The average reader then, may safely skip to chapter one leaving the rest of us to enjoy ourselves, and to wonder why on earth I have not mentioned So-and-so.

All the museums and libraries whose help I sought gave it unstintingly, no matter how complex the request or how much extra work it entailed for them. My sincere thanks are therefore due to many kind people in the following institutions: Barber Institute of Fine Arts, Birmingham; Blenheim Palace; Bodleian Library, Oxford; City Museum and Art Gallery, Birmingham; Brighton Art Gallery and Museum; Department of Drama, The University of Bristol; British Drama League; British Museum; London Museum; National Gallery of Scotland; National Maritime Museum; National Portrait Gallery; Theatre Department of New York Public Library; The University of Nottingham; Victoria and Albert Museum; Walker Art Gallery, Liverpool.

In particular I am indebted to the staff of the Theatre Section, Department of Prints and Drawings in the Victoria and Albert Museum. Mr George Nash and his assistant Mr Tony Latham have treated me with great kindness, patience and courtesy for many years. Both of them found time to read the book in typescript and made some most helpful suggestions. They have my sincere thanks.

In Staffordshire, every time I visited the City Museum and Art Gallery of Hanley, Stoke-on-Trent, Mr Arnold Mountford and Mr Gordon Elliott spared me many hours of their time and I owe them both a debt of gratitude. Their information was of great interest and help to me. Mr Elliott not only checked my technical facts but gave up some of his free time to drive me to places of interest in the Potteries in his own car.

In London all the staff of the London Library and in particular Mr Douglas Mathews have been extremely helpful.

Mr Parry Michael, Headmaster of Newport High School and Staffordshire collector extraordinary, made some very practical and interesting suggestions.

He also very kindly undertook to revise my spelling about which he was un-necessarily gentle. 'I am bound to admit that I find your spelling occasionally distinctive and original,' he wrote, and went on to explain why he felt that *cruci-fiction* 'would delight atheists but shock churchmen'.

On many pages of my notebooks throughout the years I find the initials M & M quoted as my source of information. Mr Raymond Mander and Mr Joe Mitchenson have possibly the finest private theatre collection in the world and have always been extremely helpful. Mr Peter Norwood's knowledge of nineteenth-century opera has been invaluable and in this field too I must thank Mr Vivian Liff.

In America both Miss Helen D. Willard of Harvard College Library Theatre Collection and Mrs Robin Craven in New York have been kind and helpful as has the Reference and Research Section of the United States Embassy in London.

Until his death in 1967 Mr Thomas Balston was unfailingly interested in all my research and his advice and experience were always available to me. My own copy of his book *Staffordshire Portrait Figures of the Victorian Age*, first published in 1958, is dog-eared and much respected. Where my research has tended to disprove some of his early conclusions, which I feel could perhaps mislead new collectors, I have said so. Nevertheless the greater part of this pioneer work is extremely accurate and it remains his best testimonial. All collectors of Victorian Staffordshire figures are in his debt.

Apart from Balston I have found one other book extremely useful, *Staffordshire Chimney Ornaments* by Reginald G. Haggar, published in 1955. It covers more than the Victorian period but it is a mine of accurate information. Mr Haggar gave me a whole day of his time and answered all my questions patiently, courteously and fully. All errors are, of course, my own.

It is difficult to express my thanks to Surgeon Captain P. D. G. Pugh, whose book *Staffordshire Portrait Figures and Allied Subjects of the Victorian Era* is now published. We have enjoyed sharing each other's discoveries for many years and from no one have I received more help. Although we have always worked closely together, we neither of us read the other's book until they were finished. In the letter which he sent with the proofs of his book Captain Pugh wrote: 'You may make use of anything you like—and in fact I would be delighted.' Such generosity is rare indeed. As it happens the books cover different aspects of the subject and are thus complementary to each other. The most important part of Pugh's book is the catalogue, an impressive piece of scholarship which must now inevitably replace Balston's as the standard work for many years to come.

No one can write or do accurate research if he is hungry or has indigestion; and so, although I do not know their names, I thank the staff of the canteen and res-taurant in the Victoria and Albert Museum, especially the lady who gives me a middle piece of steak-and-kidney pie with extra gravy, and all of them for their smiles. The ladies in the canteen at the British Museum I forgive, their working conditions are so appalling I feel they are not to be blamed.

My thanks are also due to Miss Jean Anderson; *The Antique Dealer and Collectors Guide*; Blakeney Art Pottery; Mr and Mrs R. Bonnett; Mr Richard Bonynge; Mr Michael Codron; *The Connoisseur*; Crispins Restaurant; Mrs Thornley Gibson; Dr Michael Gilks; Mr Douglas Hall; Mr John Hall and Mr David MacWilliams; Mrs D. Joyce and the late Mr E. H. Joyce; Mr John S. Kent; The Keystone Pottery; Punch; Mr Harry Ryans; Mr Ian Trigger; Mr and Mrs Paul Warner; Messrs Wengers Ltd, potters merchants, Stoke-on-Trent; and to my publishers Messrs William Heinemann Ltd, with special thanks to Mr Timothy Manderson for his enthusiasm and kindness.

Finally I must thank my partner, Mr Peter Sutton, without whose help, advice and encouragement this book could not have been written. He undertook to type the entire book more than once and it is only fair to add that I believe some of the spelling mistakes were his. Nevertheless his specialist knowledge of the Victorian Staffordshire figure has been invaluable and to him I owe my greatest debt.

July 1971

ANTHONY OLIVER

☙ I ❧

Setting the Scene

If we are to know more about nineteenth-century Staffordshire figures we must try to set them in their own background. They are such products of their time that they are inseparable from it. They are quite literally a potted history of the period, far more so than pottery figures of any age before or since. They were made by Englishmen for Englishmen, and if that sounds jingoistic, well, then, we are off to a good start, for very often that is exactly what they were.

There is a tendency in some books to allocate styles of potting to very definite periods. Individual figures may sometimes be dated by circumstantial evidence, but styles change slowly, the one merging gradually with the other. In the early decades of the century, figures with quite different characteristics were being made at the same time by different potters in Staffordshire.

The influence of potters working in the late eighteenth century continued well into the first half of the nineteenth. Potters like the famous Wood family influenced John Walton (*circa* 1780–1835) and his followers; Neo-Classicism blended more or less happily with rusticity. Walton produced religious figures as well as rustic ones, and some of the earliest patriotic subjects may reasonably be attributed to him.

3. "The Reading Maid". Obadiah Sherratt type. *c.*1830. 11 in.

2. Sheep and lambs by John Walton. *c.*1825. $3\frac{1}{2}$ in. $3\frac{1}{4}$ in. (part of a flock).

Patriotism as a theme was to be greatly developed in our Victorian era. Walton's ubiquitous stags, sheep and lambs with the bocage or stylized leafy tree behind them are familiar to everyone interested in English pottery. This potter must have produced more lambs in his day than New Zealand. Great flocks of them poured from the potteries and many are with us still (2).

Walton's contemporary Obadiah Sherratt (*circa* 1775–1846) was also influenced by some aspects of the work of the Woods. He is credited with some of the familiar bull-baiting groups and other subjects of rough bucolic humour and savagery. The bases of Sherratt-type figures are distinctive, rather like a table with four or six legs, a feature which is found very occasionally in some early Victorian figures (3).

The Neo-Classical influence of the late eighteenth century also spread into the nineteenth. A fair number of gods and goddesses continued to be made by potters like Walton, Neale, Enoch Wood and Felix Pratt (whose distinctive high-temperature colours of green, blue, orange, dull yellow and brown were copied by many others potters).

Ralph Wood senior (1715–72) has been credited with the dubious honour of making some of the first Toby Jugs, although recent research leaves room for doubt. Senior or junior, it makes little difference, someone invented them and they exist. It is purely a matter of taste but, to my mind, with very few exceptions they all look depressingly alike. Ralph Wood's son, grandson, and nephew, not to mention countless other potters, continued to make them with dogged persistence until the end of their potting days. They are still being made; even as I write it's a fair bet that someone in Staffordshire is making a Toby Jug. If all the Toby Jugs ever made in England were to be placed side by side, the nightmare mantel-shelf would undoubtedly encircle the globe. It is an unhappy picture, as en masse they have a distressing tendency to look like a convention of elderly female traffic wardens.

Josiah Wedgwood (1730–95) hung over the second half of his century like a great cloud of black basaltes. A hard-working man of undoubted talent, he was not entirely to blame for the sentimental Neo-Classical revival of his day. In fact there is some evidence to suggest that he would have resisted it had he not been guided by the taste of his partner Thomas Bentley, who moved in more fashionable society. Under Bentley's influence and that of friends like Sir William Hamilton, the husband of Nelson's Emma, the partnership reflected the taste of the aristocracy. It is curious that although Nelson inspired many Staffordshire potters, both in his lifetime and later in our Victorian period, the influence of his mistress's husband was to last longer.

The subjects listed in Wedgwood's Etruria factory catalogue read like a cross between the *Almanach de Gotha* and *Who's Who on Olympus*. He had earlier, in the Ivy House period, produced some of the finest creamware to come out of Stafford-

4. Typical Neo-Classical figure of the first quarter of the 19th century. Tallest $10\frac{3}{4}$ in.

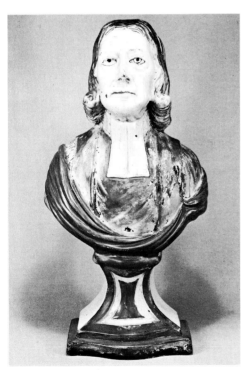

5. John Wesley. Originally modelled from life by Enoch Wood in 1781. Many later versions were made right up to the Great Exhibition in 1851. This one was made about 1830. $10\frac{1}{4}$ in.

6. Elijah and the ravens. Finely modelled Staffordshire porcelain. c.1825. 10 in.

shire, but with Bentley his taste was the taste of the Age of Reason gone berserk. He was a good enough business man to know the value of sponsorship and honestly admitted that he thought 'fashion infinitely superior to merit'. Mercifully he made very few figures, but there can be no doubt that his influence upon some of his contemporaries, such as Neale and Palmer, was considerable.

How much our figures were a conscious rebellion against Wedgwood's mar-moreal flood must remain speculative. Taste then, as now, defies accurate analysis, broad trends may be detected and certain influences seen to be at work, but only accurately in retrospect. People know what they like, but they are not always aware of their reasons at the time.

Josiah Wedgwood still has many admirers and there is nothing more formidable than your Wedgwood dealer or collector. I've been backed into many a corner and lectured by them – the ladies are far more aggressive than the men – but it has done nothing to make me love it more. Nothing surprises me less than that the rocks brought back from the dead surface of the moon contain large amounts of black basaltes. The fact that a growing number of collectors is beginning to love the dotty gaiety of the Victorian figures will be of interest to art historians of the future. No doubt they will point out that some aspects of modern art may well have echoed those splendid, anonymous, back-street potters of Staffordshire.

All these varied styles appeared in the first forty years of the nineteenth century. On mantel-shelves all over England sheep and lambs were protected by slightly hyperthyroid shepherds and shepherdesses. "The Four Seasons" jostled for atten-tion with "Diana and Apollo"; "Faith, Hope and Charity" bore silent witness to the liberality of "Ceres and Pomona", while "Andromache" mourned interminably over the ashes of Hector. Village boys and girls demurely displayed their proficiency in reading, not daring to raise their eyes to the sour-faced gaze of "John Wesley". Bulls were baited, and sailors said Farewell, but Returned in time to take their place beside "Elijah" and the "Widow of Zarapeth" (4, 5 and 6).

It should be remembered that although the Industrial Revolution and the consequent drift to the towns may be said to have dated effectively from the mid eighteenth century, England was still essentially a rural society. The twenty-year war with Revolutionary and Napoleonic France (1793–1815) wrought changes, but they came gradually. Living conditions in the expanding, largely unplanned towns were bad, though not nearly so bad as they were to become later in the century. The purchasing power of wages, however, for most workers, was greater than it had been just before the war. More money led to a demand for luxuries, including pottery of all kinds, and it was in these conditions that the taste of the early nineteenth century developed. If you longed for the half-remembered country scenes of your childhood, then a mantel-shelf meadow with Walton sheep was the next best thing. If you envied the rich their Chelsea and Derby and Meissen, your

7. Staffordshire porcelain. *c.*1835. 7 in.

pocket could afford cheap imitations, even if they had feet of clay.

By the beginning of the century the coloured glazes of the early Wood figures had mostly given way to the low-temperature enamel colours of his successors. Enamel colours could be used in a greater range than had been possible before, but on the whole it is the rather subdued greens and browns that dominate the palette of the pre-Victorian figures. There are occasional flashes of brighter colours, but even with these the relatively non-reflective surface of the enamel tends to produce a muted effect. The high-temperature colours of Felix Pratt and his imitators, however, are different and distinctive, a bright oasis in an otherwise rather dull desert. There is no doubt that some of these early nineteenth-century figures have great charm, and current prices show that they remain popular with many collectors. For my own taste they are perhaps too derivative, too busy in an unsuccessful attempt to imitate the porcelain style of Chelsea and Derby.

Round about 1820 one small but important group of figures appears which is so completely different from the ones discussed above that some authorities have dated them as 1840–45. They undoubtedly share many of the characteristics of the early Victorian figures, including a whiter body clay (which was sometimes porcellaneous), occasional use of the famous underglaze cobalt blue, and some gold decoration. Research I did when I was trying to identify some of these figures now leads me to believe that they must be the fore-runners of our Victorian figures and yet another example of the blurred demarcation line between styles.

5

Not only were they different in style and palette, but they owed nothing to the eighteenth century for inspiration. Many of them appear to be the portraits of actors and actresses. Curiously enough the theatre, which was to prove such a source of inspiration for the potters, had been slow to fire their imagination. The eighteenth century had produced some theatrical subjects, but nothing like the numbers which were to follow later. In the nineteenth century before Victoria ascended the throne, it was to the theatre that the new-style potters turned in the transitionary period.

The praying figure of "Madame Vestris" (1797–1856) is of some importance in establishing the style of these earlier figures because it is possible to be reasonably accurate about the exact date.

The novel *Paul et Virginie*, written by that disciple of Rousseau, Bernardin de St-Pierre, was first published in 1787. It is a rather sentimental story of a young French boy and girl brought up together on the island of Mauritius, far from civilization. Virginie returns to France for a few years at the command of a rich relative. Her return, so long awaited by Paul, is disastrous. The ship is wrecked by a hurricane within sight of Paul on the shore; he tries to rescue her and fails. When begged by a naked sailor to strip off and allow herself to be saved, Virginie, with what can only be described as an excess of delicacy, refuses and drowns. Paul dies of grief shortly after.

As *Paul and Virginia* the novel had enormous popularity in England almost to the end of the nineteenth century and was adapted for the stage many times. One of the earliest of these was a musical version by James Cobb which was produced for the first time on 1 May 1800 at Covent Garden. Madame Vestris made her first professional appearance on the stage on 19 February 1820, and two years later, on 26 January 1822, now establishing herself as a star, she played Paul in Cobb's musical version at Drury Lane with great success. The one vital difference between the novel and Cobb's adaptation was that Cobb, either because of the difficulty of presenting a naked sailor on the stage, or simply because he disliked tragedy, gave it a happy ending. The final curtain descends with Paul giving thanks on his knees for Virginia's safe deliverance from the shipwreck. '*From the cruel waves, Fate the fair Virginia saves.*'

The figure (8) is unmistakably female and I can find no record of Vestris, or indeed any other actress, playing the part before or after 1822. Although no exact print of this final scene seems to exist, there are prints of Vestris as Paul, and the costume is almost identical. It seems reasonable therefore to regard this figure, with its white porcellaneous body, its deep underglaze cobalt blue jacket, and fine gold decoration, as dating from *circa* 1822.

Another fine pre-Victorian figure may be seen in 9. Thomas Potter Cooke (1786–1864) was one of the most famous stage sailors of all time. His characteriza-

8. Madame Vestris as Paul, 1822. 6¾ in.

9. Thomas Potter Cooke dancing his famous hornpipe. c.1825. 10½ in.

tion and the way he danced the hornpipe were authentic. He had served in the Royal Navy as a boy and seen active service including the battle of Cape St Vincent in 1797. His first stage appearance was in 1804 and his last at Covent Garden in 1860. He could pack a theatre when even Macready, Kemble or Siddons failed. His most famous part was William, the sailor hero in *Black Ey'd Susan*, first produced at the Surrey Theatre on 8 June 1829. No one had seen a real sailor quite like Cooke on the stage before and his hornpipe dance was a sensation.

Like Vestris, Cooke is modelled in the round and shares all the same characteristics of colour and body. The true transitional nature of this interesting period may be seen in the way some other famous actors were presented. Sometimes the modelling is very similar, like the figure of Thomas Dartmouth Rice (1806–60) the American actor who was one of the first to impersonate a negro character

10. 'Turn about an' wheel about an' do jis so, An ebery time I turn about I jump Jim Crow'. Thomas Dartmouth Rice at the Surrey Theatre, 1836. $5\frac{3}{4}$ in.

11. This same print was also used on theatre posters in the provinces to advertise John Scott (Little Scott) as 'Jim Crow'. (By courtesy of the Victoria and Albert Museum.)

(10). He sang his most famous song, 'Jump Jim Crow', at the Surrey Theatre in 1836, just a year before Victoria's accession, and yet the potters used only enamel colours for the figure. Perhaps they felt that rags and tatters would look odd with a lustrous cobalt-blue jacket (11).

Pure cobalt oxide was expensive, and as early as 1802 Thénard, a French chemist, had invented a much cheaper way of using it with little loss of brilliance. However the potters do not appear to have realized the full possibilities of Thénard's discovery until our period begins in earnest with Victoria's reign.

So style and palette evolved slowly; but just as important was the potters' growing awareness of the world around them. That is the real significance of these

12. 'Her Majesty has been on horseback almost every day throughout the week'.
Bells Life in London and Sporting Chronicle, 30 September 1838 (*c*.1840. 8 in.)

9

pre-Victorian figures. Just as the eighteenth-century bocage figures of Chelsea and Derby had influenced the Walton school, the nineteenth-century figures of Derby and Rockingham were reflected in our pre-Victorian Staffordshire figures which appear about 1820, but with a difference. The Walton school was crude – which was part of its charm – but no one could ever have mistaken its figures for porcelain; they remained unashamedly earthenware. The new group of figures, however, were sometimes of an extremely high quality and, being of a porcellaneous body, competed with Derby and Rockingham on much higher terms. They could be – and often were – attributed to both factories, and this situation exists to this day, causing endless trouble and confusion among collectors and dealers alike. Both Derby and Rockingham made theatrical figures (sometimes almost identical apart from the factory mark), and the chief modeller of Derby theatre figures, Samuel Keyes, is known to have left there and gone to Staffordshire in 1826.

It was natural that the theatre should be the catalyst for it was becoming increasingly important in the lives of the people. London in 1800 had only nine theatres; by 1840 the number had risen to over sixty. A similar pattern could be seen in the new industrial centres all over England. As more and more workers were forced into the muck and stench of the unplanned towns by the late tide of the Industrial Revolution, the demand for entertainment grew, and created new gods and goddesses. Madame Vestris had ousted Minerva, and in doing so had established a new age and a new style. It seems only fitting that one of her greatest successes was to be called *Olympic Revels*.

The theatre produced great stars at that time but they couldn't compete with Queen Victoria. There is a story told of how Queen Mary, who loved the theatre, visited the Strand Theatre to see Lilian Braithwaite and Mary Jerrold in *Arsenic and Old Lace*. The two stars peeped through holes in the curtain to watch Queen Mary, blazing with diamonds, enter her box and graciously acknowledge the applause of the audience. 'What an entrance!' said Mary Jerrold, wistfully. 'What a part!' said Lilian Braithwaite, who was more practical.

It is true, it was a magnificent part and it always has been. You have only to watch our present Queen meeting stars at a film première to realize that in comparison, poor loves, they don't stand a chance.

The potters of Staffordshire were quick to seize their opportunity, and the trumpets that heralded Victoria's reign also proclaimed the beginning of our period.

The People Who Made Them

England in the middle of the nineteenth century: supremely confident, powerful, smug, battered by sopranos and cholera, wisely allying herself to God to hold dominion over half the world, hanging murderers in public, working children to death in private, but mercifully with the non-conformist liberal worm worrying her guts, servile and sentimental, an age when forelocks and hearts were touched with equal facility.

At the beginning of Victoria's reign the area of the Staffordshire Potteries was not yet the seething, unplanned, urban mess that it was to become later in the century. It was still possible to separate the different townships and to find farms and green fields between them. The Vale of Trent was still beautiful with clean flowing water. The worst ravages of the Industrial Revolution were not seen until you entered the towns themselves, where the water running in the streets came from the overflowing cesspits. There was great squalor, poverty, human misery, and some happiness.

From contemporary evidence and later accounts it is possible to follow a worker through a typical day. He rose at 5 a.m. and walked through leafy lanes one and a half miles to the pot-bank in the town, 'a rambling ramshackle conglomeration of buildings as if a stampede of cottages had been arrested in their march'. The various workshops which made up the tiny factory were dotted about with no sense of order at different levels, so that some of them were below the surface of the uneven ground, 'always damp and with little light, even at midsummer'.

This worker's first job was to light the fire in some of the ovens and drying stoves so that work could start at 6 a.m. He was a mould-runner, carrying a heavy load of moulds containing the damp clay figures across an open yard into the drying-room. In winter the yard was often freezing, but the drying-room was always about 120 degrees Fahrenheit (50 degrees centigrade), summer and winter. In 1840, in what must have been one of the first ever 'time and motion' studies, he carried in an average day 3,840 pounds a total distance of 7 miles, 1,120 yards. In the rare times during the day when there was nothing ready for him to carry, he was occupied in 'wedging' clay. He raised the heavy lumps of raw clay above his head and crashed them down over and over again on to a wooden bench with all his strength to expel as many air bubbles as possible (13 and 14).

He had half an hour at 9 a.m. for breakfast, which was bread or sometimes stir pudding, a kind of crude porridge, warmed on the stove in the drying-room. His

13. Beating the clay to make it solid, smooth and pliable fit for the Potter.

14. Placing the "dipped" ware ready for its being fired or baked in the "Glazing" Oven.

dinner time was from 1 p.m. to 2 p.m. and was stir pudding again. He finished his day at 8 or 9 p.m. and walked the long journey back to his home, sometimes sleeping as he walked. At home he had his first food since midday, potatoes, and sometimes a little bacon or beef. His wages were a shilling a week and he was seven years old.

Nothing in that account of a child's working day in the Staffordshire Potteries is invented; much of it was taken from official records in the State Paper Room at the British Museum. It is by no means an exceptional case. Children were employed extensively in the Potteries and the early twinges of Victorian conscience prompted the *Report of the Royal Commission on Children's Employment in Industry* in 1843. In fact the report covers workers of all ages, not only children; and some knowledge of it is essential to a fuller understanding of the figures. The superb primitive art which came from these people is of the people themselves, and to know nothing of them puts a collector at a disadvantage. A Staffordshire potter whose name is forgotten wrote these lines:

No art with Potters can compare
We make our pots of what we Potters are.

Gentlemen,

I have the honour to lay before you the evidence that I have collected relating to the physical and moral condition of the children labouring in the important district of the Staffordshire Potteries which comprise the parishes and townships of Stoke-upon-Trent, Longton, Fenton, Burslem, Lane Delph, Hanley, Shelton,

12

15. *c.*1846. 8½ in.

16. *c.*1846. 7½ in.

Cobridge, Longport and Tunstall, extending from north to south a distance of nine miles, of unequal breadth or from one to three miles, and having a population of 70,000 souls chiefly of the working classes.

So wrote Samuel Scrivens, Her Majesty's Commissioner, reporting to both Houses of Parliament in 1843. I don't doubt that he was glad to lay down his pen and hoped that some good might come of it, for Scrivens seems to have been a kind man, honest and impartial. He visited all grades of factory from the largest to the smallest. His evidence was taken when our figures are about to start their best period and gives us a unique contemporary view.

The opening lines of this chapter are not merely intended as an exercise in rhetoric, they could well stand as a condensed catalogue of the back-street potters' output, for they reflect their interests faithfully and mention nothing which escaped their attention. For all workers, hours of labour and working conditions were appalling, but there is some evidence to show that the very smallest pot-banks were

13

sometimes happier places to work in than the larger factories. Small units tended to work almost as a family group, avoiding the casual cruelties and immoralities so common in the others. If it is true that there was a demand for the figures from a new public, it is also true that the workers who made them were poorly paid and badly organized. With Sir Robert Peel at the Home Office, Pitt's Combination Act of 1800, which prevented combinations of workers against their masters, was repealed in 1825 and trade unions became legal. Peel's place in the affections of the potters was further assured because he had the courage to change his mind and repeal the hated Corn Laws which had caused so much suffering amongst the poor. They loved Cobden for influencing Peel's decision (15) (16).

On the whole the Trade Union movement in the Potteries was a miserable failure, 'haphazard, feebly and timidly followed'. The potters were too individual and, unlike the mechanized mills of Lancashire, the Potteries were basically a cottage industry writ large. But they depended on coal for their existence and the colliers' strike of 1842 stopped all the pot-banks like the slam of a door. A series of strikes by the potters themselves produced some marginal improvements, but at a great cost. After the strike of 1836–7 many of them lost their homes, and the movement was side-tracked into a disastrous scheme to raise funds to buy land in America. The idea was to deprive the masters of surplus workers and thus give a greater bargaining power to those who remained. Workers and their families for this great adventure were to be chosen by lottery, and so great was the enthusiasm that even the name of the new town in America was proudly announced. It was to be called Pottersville.

In February 1846 a small advance party of 'Land Officers' and their families set sail for New York. Obeying the traditional call to the West they got as far as Wisconsin, where they wandered around the prairies for weeks on end, looking for someone in authority with power to sell land. Sleeping under the stars, getting lost in forests and bumping into Red Indians in the dark – if the story were not so pathetic it would come close to farce. Eventually 1,200 acres of land was sold to them, and a slow trickle of by now reluctant immigrants came to join them. With constant bickering and lack of money the ultimate fate of this original land is obscure. It might well have been sold to enable the potters to try elsewhere, for there is no record of any Pottersville today in Wisconsin, although Pennsylvania has both a Pottersville and a Pottsville. This wildcat scheme, which destroyed their union by bleeding it of funds, shone like a star in their eyes for five or six years before it was finally abandoned.

For a long time I wondered why the potters chose to make a figure of William Penn (17), but The Emigration Society would seem to supply a possible answer. I suspect that the sealed deeds in his hand are not only, as Balston thought, 'the letters patent for his American lands', but also a symbol for the land the potters

17. William Penn, Quaker and founder of Pennsylvania. *c*.1846. 8¼ in. In the collection of Mr Patrick Gibson. Photograph by courtesy of Surgeon Captain P. D. G. Pugh.

had bought for themselves. Some of these figures of Penn must have gone to America with the emigrants, and perhaps some have survived over there, but most of them would have been placed on the mantel-shelves of hopeful investors in England as a symbol of faith for a new life in a better world.

No wonder they tried to get away. Traditionally a working potter was hired for a year at Martinmas (11 November). He was expected to give twopence, three-pence or even fourpence in the shilling back to his master. The Truck Act of 1831 made it illegal to pay a worker in goods instead of money, but the system died hard, and a roll of cloth or a cheap piece of Birmingham jewellery was poor comfort for empty stomachs. A potter was paid only for figures 'good from the oven', whether the fault was his or not. This was one of his biggest grievances, for he had no means of knowing if he had been cheated. With a weak and almost useless union to protect him he lived his life as best he could, and if he could not change his masters' rules, he made his own. Sometimes he would not work on Monday or Tuesday and stop-ped at midday on Saturday. A worker doing so was said to be 'at play'. For the

CAUTION

TO

PERSONS TIPPLING,

AND TO

PUBLICANS.

THE UNDERSIGNED MANUFACTURERS of Earthen-Ware within the parish of BURSLEM, sustaining the most serious loss and inconvenience, by daily interruptions to their business, in consequence of the habits of idleness and tippling which many of their workmen indulge in, during the regular hours of work, and in which they find encouragement by the very CULPABLE CONDUCT OF MANY PUBLICANS within this parish; Do hereby make known, that from the publication of this Notice, *they are resolved to give every protection and support to such persons as will lay complaints before the Magistrates, against any workmen for the offence of tippling ;* and the undersigned Manufacturers have also resolved,

Individually to notice and to report to the Magistrates

The conduct of all such Publicans as shall from henceforth suffer any workmen to remain tippling in their houses during the regular working hours, or at any other improper time.

THE PUBLICANS ARE HEREBY INFORMED,

That on conviction of the offence of suffering tippling, or unlawful Games in their houses, they are liable to *forfeit their recognizances,* and to have their *licenses suspended* for the space of *three years,* besides being subject to a penalty of ten shillings for every offence by tippling ; and that *the Magistrates acting for this Hundred have come to the resolution of putting these laws strictly in force for the future.*

☞ Any person found tippling in a Public-house is liable to a penalty of three shillings and four-pence, to the use of the Poor, besides the costs of the information.

Burslem, November, 1815.

Wood & Caldwell	Jno. & Rich. Riley	Jno. Rogers
Henshall & Williamsons	Tho. & Benj. Godwin	Rhead & Goodfellow
Jno. & Jas. Davenport	William Stanley	Machin & Co.
Thomas Heath	John Brettell	Wm. Bourne & Co.
Samuel Tomkinson	William Moseley	James Cartlidge
Ralph Johnson	Stevenson and Bucknall	J. and R. Blackwell
Thomas Bathwell	Wm. Walsh	Benj. Godwin and Sons
Edward Bourne	John Haywood	F. and N. Dillon
John & Christr. Robinson	John Wood	Ralph Stevenson
John Hall	Lindop & Taylor	R. and J. Clews

* Every Publican within this parish will be expected to keep one of these Notices conspicuously posted up in his house, as a proof he is determined to maintain good order therein.

TREGORTHA, PRINTER.

18. By courtesy of The City Museum and Art Gallery, Stoke-on-Trent.

16

rest of the week, to make up his quota, he worked 'like a galley slave' far into the night. A Mr Richard Dudson, who had risen from the bench to become master of his own pot-bank, opened his heart to Mr Scrivens and, with all of two and a half years as an employer behind him, was suddenly seeing things in a new light:

'I have not the least doubt that I should prosper greatly if I could depend upon the working hours of the men. . . . if I had been a provident man and worked when I could I should have been better off now and so would many others.'

(*Commission Report.*)

Many of the children were not employed direct but were hired by working potters as assistants, so that they had to work the same hours, however late. Drink kept some of the men going; the child's stimulant was more often a flogging with a rope caked in hard clay. Outside drinking in working hours was forbidden by the masters (18), and the children were sent to smuggle it in for the men. Occasionally an all-night orgy of drink and sex would ensue, leaving a number of very sorry, and possibly wiser, women and girls painting some rather shaky flowers the next day.

Joseph Booth, aged nine, started work when he was seven. He was paid two shillings and threepence a week and his brother a shilling.

'I bring breakfast with me, it is stir pudding, I go home for dinner and get stir pudding and stir pudding for supper. I get home at eight or nine and come at six. I get cold. I would sooner work thirteen hours than fifteen.' This child was literally in rags.

(*Commission Report.*)

George Guest was eleven and finished work at 6 p.m. on Mondays and 8.30 p.m. for the rest of the week.

'I should like a play in the yard but cannot have it. . . . When I get home my legs ache and I am too tired to play then but get my supper and go to bed. I would rather work ten hours than fourteen but if I was to get less money I would rather work late and get more beef.'

(*Commission Report.*)

Elizabeth Evans, aged eleven.

'I got bread this morning for breakfast, bread for dinner, I don't know what I shall have for tea, perhaps taties. . . . I have nothing to complain of.'

(*Commission Report.*)

No machinery could make the figures. The modellers were the unknown artists; the children were often the machinery. Robert Moreton, aged nine, was a figure-

17

maker for his father, William Moreton.

'I work by the piece and can make forty dozen small figures a day. I get a penny for ten dozen, that is about two shillings a week. I work from seven to seven, sometimes eight or nine.'

(Commission Report.)

William Cotton, aged nine.

'I can complete three and a half dozen pieces in the hour and earn two shillings a week.'

(Commission Report.)

Perhaps the most touching evidence of all was that of Jane Lea, aged nine.

'I am a painter . . .'
This child was so diffident I could get nothing from her.

(Commission Report.)

On the whole the girls and women who did the painting and decorating had better working conditions than the other workers. Even so, the quality of the painting can vary a great deal and should always be taken into account when assessing the merits of a figure. The original modeller is our true artist, and apart from him, and the painters, the other workers were no more than the hand of a printing-press operator who turns out a limited edition of an original Picasso. Pregnant women worked until the last possible moment and then returned to work, leaving their new-born children with the 'child minders' who mostly spent the money given to them on drink, and fed the children with bread dipped in water so that few of them survived. Those who did, stayed at home alone as toddlers, with open unprotected fires burning the fierce Staffordshire coal, and a number were burnt to death every year.

In the sagger house the unfired dry figures were packed in the sagger on a bed of ground flint to steady them for their first firing in the biscuit oven. A 'sagger' is a case of baked fireproof clay enclosing pottery while it is being dried and later fired. (It is probably a contraction of the word 'safeguard'.) When they emerged from the biscuit oven the figures were 'brushed' with sandpaper and stone to remove chips and prominent mould seams, so that the air was thick with sharp siliceous dust as fine as flour. This air in the scouring room was a killer and they knew it ('we all feel overloaded upon the chest'). But even more dangerous was to work as a dipper in the glazing room.

The figures were dipped by hand into the poisonous liquid lead glaze. Glaze recipes varied from bank to bank, but all contained lead and sometimes arsenic, which was a good flux. Dippers died of lead poisoning; their clothes and arms up to

19. "Pressing" or "Squeezing", which is making jugs turenes &c. of the clay ready for being fired.

20. Painting and Gilding China or Earthenware.

21. "Glazing" or dipping the ware in a prepared liquid, which produces the glossy surface.

22. Examining and dressing the ware after its coming from the potters and glazing ovens.

the elbows were constantly soaked in it. There were no washrooms and they ate their food in the same room. It caused anaemia, colic, muscular paralysis which first affected their fingers and hands and then spread to involve the whole body. Other horrible symptoms were mental disturbances and convulsions, especially in children, chronic constipation and blindness. Men dippers were paid about thirty-two shillings a week and boys five shillings, 'for the risk they run'. The emotive word, arsenic, held more terrors for them than lead. They were told that the glaze contained no arsenic, which may have been true, 'but we have our own ideas about that, it destroys our health, we work off the effects with opening medicine frequently or it would soon be all over for us'. But it was the lead that killed them just the same. It dried on their skin and clothing and was inhaled as dust or ingested with their food. They carried it back to their homes and poisoned their families (19, 20, 21 and 22).

Mr J. Harding, Medical Officer, Hanley, Stoke-on-Trent:

'I am not aware that there is anything particularly calculated to produce disease amongst children in the manufacture of earthenware and porcelain, nor are their hours of labour so very long as to preclude the possibility of their taking sufficient exercise out of doors.'

(*Commission Report.*)

Sanitary conditions were bad. Scrivens noted that

in eight cases out of ten the places of convenience are indecently and disgustingly exposed and filthy, girls pass through the hovels where the lowest classes of men and boys work. The shed was crudely partitioned and exposed to the gaze of half of the men.

The stink from the overflowing cesspits was everywhere; if there was a sewer it emptied into the canal which brought the barges loaded with clay.

Average Weekly Wage List, 1843

Moulders	£1	10	0
Modellers	£1	10	0
Dippers	£1	12	0
Painters & Gilders	£1	4	0
Slip Makers	£1	19	0
Oven Man	£3	0	0
Children		2	0½

(*Commission Report.*)

The oven man's wage is easy to understand when you consider that he could ruin the whole batch of figures and the other workers only one at a time. Regulating the oven temperature was a skilled and tricky job. Sometimes figures will show signs of having been fired at too high a temperature with dull enamel colours or even a bubbling on the enamel surface (23).

Although the conditions in which the figures were made may seem difficult to believe today, we would do well to remember that it was so, and to remember the

The Murder of Thomas Smith by William Collier. *c.*1866. 13½ in. See also 69.   Colour Plate 1.

23. A Potters Oven when firing or baking, the ware being therein placed in Safeguards or "Saggers".

24. Pure drinking water fountains. *c.*1861. 12 in. 11½ in.

children who may have helped to make them. The effects of such conditions have been far-reaching, right down to our own times. The greed and selfishness of some nineteenth-century employers is matched by the greed and selfishness of some unions today.

And what did they do, these men, women and children of Staffordshire, in their few short hours of leisure, or when they were 'at play'? We need to know, for their loves and hates they put into our figures. Wages for groups of workers were paid in 'notes' on Saturday, and could only be converted into money in a specified pub, which was sometimes also owned by the master. Whether they wanted to or not, to the pub they went, and an unwritten law made sure that some of the money was spent on drink before they were paid. A sovereign changed later in the week, perhaps at a grocer's shop, was always carefully weighed and usually pronounced 'light', so that they seldom got more than 19/6d. for it. Beer- and ale-houses abounded, and a father commanding the combined wages of his family, amounting perhaps to three pounds, could still let his wife and children starve. Temperance societies fought a losing battle with drink and were not much encouraged. They gained ground in the '50s and '60s, and were active in propaganda and in erecting public drinking fountains of pure water (24). Fear of cholera was another reason for the popularity of these fountains.

Pugilism (25) and dog-fighting were much-favoured sports and, if racing and hunting could only be enjoyed at a distance, the potters were happy to record

TOM LANE

JOHNNY WALKER

25. Two superb Staffordshire figures of boxers, here illustrated for the first time. Johnny Walker, born January 1817, 'a perfect Hercules in miniature', Lightweight Champion of England, was challenged by Tom Lane, born February 1825, the youngest and brightest hope of a famous family of pugilists. The prize fight, on which vast sums of money had been wagered, took place on 15 February 1848. The result occasioned one of the greatest boxing scandals of the century. Walker astounded his fans by retiring unmarked after only thirteen rounds and was generally thought to have accepted a bribe. No other examples of these figures are known. 1848. 7¼ in.

26. Huntsman and hounds in full cry. *c*.1845. 5 in.

their popularity too (26). The influence of Wesley was strong (although I have found a record of some four hundred Catholic children in the district). The towns were full of Wesley's chapels and their offshoots, The New Connection, the Christian Association, and of course the Primitive Methodists founded by their own Hugh Bourne in Stoke-on-Trent. It is curious but as far as I know there is no figure of of Hugh Bourne, a prophet without enough honour in his own country perhaps. It shows at least that the potters aimed at a wide market. The Rev. J. Bryan, the splendid, one-eyed Rev. Christmas Evans and the Rev. John Elias were obviously intended mainly for the Welsh, and the Rev. Charles Spurgeon for London (27, 28 and 29). The potters loved a good crime, as we do today, especially if it was on their own doorstep. If Hugh Bourne was ignored, then Collier and his victim Smith were potted with gusto (colour plate 1).

Few of the potters could read or write, so that any book or magazine with illustrations was very popular. They talked; they talked at work and in the ale-and-spirit houses. The most interesting news of the day filtered down from The Lamb and the hotel where the gentlemen were discussing England or the world (which was the same thing). It reached the bar parlour of The Foaming Quart, or one of

27. Rev. John Bryan. *c*.1856. 10½ in. Dr Raffles or Rev. Joseph Fletcher. *c*.1849. 9½ in.

28. Rev. Christmas Evans, ex-farm labourer. It was said that when he preached of hell fire you could feel the heat. *c*.1856. 13½ in.

29. Rev. John Wesley and Rev. Charles Spurgeon. *The Morning Post*, Monday, 18 May. 1857 considered Spurgeon to be 'probably the most popular comedian of the day'. *c*.1857. 11¼ in. 11¾ in.

30. Village Schoolboys. Based on a painting by W. Mulready, R.A. *c.*1860. 10 in.

31. Holy water stoup. *c.*1870. 16½ in.

the hundreds of other pubs where the potters were drinking, and sometimes – just sometimes – the magic worked. The great kaleidoscope of Victorian England swirled about them until an image, a tiny coloured fragment of it, froze in the mind like a frame from a cinema film. Royalty, Protestants, Catholics, actors, murderers and politicians . . . When the potters' attention was caught, the image was slapped into clay, either modelled on a convenient print, or from his imagination. Wars, battles, generals on superb horses, saints, sailors, sinners, and the lady who invented bloomers, they didn't miss a trick. (See also Chapter 5.)

And the children, what did they do in their pitifully few free hours? The very lucky ones might have a few months in a village dame school before the factory got them (30). School cost between twopence and eightpence a week, and not many got the chance. Sunday Schools were free; the teachers were mostly workers and not good, but a child could sit with a clean face in a warm room from nine to half past ten on Sunday morning and learn of the Lord who loved him (31). If

32. Victoria and Albert modelled in one of the larger Staffordshire factories. c.1843. 17½ in. 18½ in.

33. Victoria with her first-born child, the Princess Royal. 1841. 6¾ in. impressed LLOYD/SHELTON.

34. Victoria with the Princess Royal and Albert. c.1841. 7½ in.

he had the energy he could walk in green fields and look for birds' nests. When Wakes week came there was the glory of the fair and a thronged market-place with swings, hobby-horses, ginger bread, Aunt Sally, and a real live theatre made of board and canvas with 'the finest company in the world' (see also Chapter 9). These were the best of times, but they could scarcely make up for the rest.

If work failed a family there was Poor Law relief bread, full of sawdust and lumps of plaster-of-Paris, and beyond that the terror of the workhouse which separated husbands and wives and children from each other. These, then, are the potters who made our figures; this is how they lived and worked. The wonder is of course that there was no large-scale revolt. There were riots in 1842 and 1847; they burnt houses, the Riot Act was read to them and Queen Victoria's soldiers came and fired on them; some were wounded and one was killed. The workers were patriotic and, incredible though it may seem, they loved their country. They listened to the rebel leaders, and they listened to the chapels, and they went back to work and made figures of the Queen, and Albert, and the royal children.

When I was in Stoke-on-Trent doing some research for this book, I drank in a pub one night with a highly intelligent old man whose family had worked there as potters for over two hundred years.

'How could such things have happened?' I asked him.

'It was the French,' he said. 'They went too far too fast in 1790, and over here the workers were afraid of it. And then there was Wesley – the spirit of John Wesley hung over the Potteries like an avenging angel of peace – pissing on the flames of revolution.'

The English are a remarkable people.

35. Victoria and Albert with their first two children, Prince of Wales and Princess Royal. *c*.1846. $9\frac{3}{4}$ in. $10\frac{1}{2}$ in.

36. Royal children. *c*.1845. $4\frac{1}{2}$ in.

37. Royal children. *c*.1845. $7\frac{1}{2}$ in. Some versions are more finely modelled with a separate wheel.

3

What They are Made of

If this book is to be of some practical help to collectors of Victorian Staffordshire figures, then it is necessary not only to know something of how they evolved in style, but also of the materials with which they were made.

I know very well, from the questions new collectors ask me, that they find it extremely difficult to understand the differences between the numerous clay bodies with which our figures were made. Indeed many of them had no idea that such differences existed, for most books which mention Victorian Staffordshire figures refer to them simply as Staffordshire Pottery and leave it at that. I hope that this chapter will help to clarify the position.

Some 'Staffordshire' pottery was not made in Staffordshire, and some of it is not pottery. Scottish potteries made figures that are very like Staffordshire – which is not surprising, as many of their workers came from the potteries of Staffordshire. In practice comparatively few of these figures appear on the market and they need not concern us here.

Almost all the figures with which we are concerned were made in the relatively small area of North Staffordshire known as the Potteries – the famous 'six towns' of Tunstall, Burslem, Hanley, Fenton, Longton and Stoke. No other area in England has known such a concentrated production of pottery and porcelain for so long a

38. "Blending" or mixing the materials with water, forming a Compound called Slip.

39. "Boiling the Slip" to evaporate the water, leaving a clay about the consistence of dough.

KEEPER'S NEW LODGE, AND DOG-KENNEL, WINDSOR.

40. The Queen had this cottage built in May 1843 for Mr Maynard, the keeper of the royal pet dogs. *Illustrated London News*, June 1843. (New Source)

41. Windsor Lodge. Staffordshire porcelain, often sold as Rockingham. *c*.1843. $5\frac{1}{4}$ in.

period. At the City Museum of Stoke-on-Trent I was told that the Potteries are, in effect, one vast shard pit filled with the wasters of centuries, and that even the roads are built on crushed pottery for drainage. A waster is a piece of pottery spoiled or flawed in manufacture. The earliest examples in the museum date from the fifteenth century. There are ample deposits of different quality clays, a good supply of water and, perhaps most important of all, rich coal fields.

Now the danger of discussing the technical background of our figures is that it could so easily develop into a finger-wagging, boring lecture with a mass of superfluous ceramic data. When I started to read through my first draft of this chapter I was really rather proud of it. It was, I thought, an accurate and succinct account of the history of ceramics – starting modestly in ancient China and working its way through Italy, Germany and France, and thereafter reinforcing the native art of Staffordshire by way of Plymouth, Bristol, Bow, Chelsea, Derby and Fulham. Round about page nine I started to get the giggles because, although I truly had tried to keep my natural pomposity under control, the whole thing had got wildly out of hand. Here was a right old farrago of fictile flag-waving, a positive plethora of pedantry (and most of it pinched to boot). Nevertheless it is important to know something of the different bodies used by our potters. Nothing puzzles a new collector more than to be told that a figure is porcelain and not pottery, especially when to the uninformed eye they are identical. So let us try and get that cleared up once and for all, and I promise to stick to basics and the things which worried me when I began to collect.

30

The body of figures made in Staffordshire in the eighteenth century was comparatively simple. They were made of earthenware and various forms of stoneware. Most books which mention Victorian figures at all refer to them as pottery or earthenware and this is not accurate. By the time our figures were made in the nineteenth century a far greater number of bodies were available to the potter. In addition to earthenware the following bodies were also used: porcelain, semi-porcelain, and bone china. The common constituent of all these bodies is clay. So much at least is simple.

Most people know what clay looks like in its natural state. If they haven't broken their backs digging a clay soil garden, they must have slipped on it at some time or other and gone flying. Anyone who has done so will have revealed two of its chief characteristics, its extreme malleability, and its property of retaining an accurate impression. If the Young Lady of Gloucester was eventually traced by her parents, their thanks were almost certainly due to a bed of clay lying immediately below the surface of the grass.

If clay is baked in an oven it undergoes a chemical change and sets hard, being then known as earthenware or pottery. It is porous and opaque. Take this process a stage further and submit the clay to an extreme heat and it becomes vitrified, or changed into a glass-like non-porous substance, and is called stoneware. If a suitable amount of a more easily fusible material is added to the clay, a lower temperature will produce the same result. Stoneware is really a sort of halfway house between pottery and porcelain, having some of the properties of both. It is, for example, very slightly translucent if potted thinly enough, but in thicker areas will not transmit light. The fundamental difference between earthenware and porcelain is that the latter is always translucent to a greater or lesser degree and the former is always opaque.

Just as pottery and earthenware are synonymous, so are porcelain and china. If a fine white clay and a certain kind of decomposed granite rock called china stone (both of which are found in Cornwall) are fired together at the correct temperature the result is a true hard-paste porcelain such as was made originally in China. The so-called soft-paste porcelain produced by most of the famous English factories, Bow, Chelsea, Derby, etc., was an attempt to imitate this hard-paste body. Frit or powdered glass was added to the white clay, and this fused at a much lower temperature. Sometimes different amounts of calcined ox-bones were added to give it greater stability in the oven. The potter who first developed this technique on a large scale was Josiah Spode. When he added the calcined ox-bones to his new porcelain formula the result was the famous English bone china. All these porcelains are translucent to a greater or lesser degree.

Porcelain, both the hard paste and the more beautiful soft paste, had come to England in the eighteenth century and by the year 1800 both were known in

42. Protestantism and Popery. Fine heavy earthenware in the tradition of porcelain by Thomas Parr. *c.*1851. 9 in. 9½ in.

Staffordshire, as was bone china. The differences between pottery and porcelain are obvious, yet the dividing line is vague and difficult to define accurately. From the melting pot of the Staffordshire ovens were to come dozens of hybrids. Clays mixed with ground-up stones, flint, and dozens of other secret ingredients were all to be lumped unceremoniously under the generic title of Staffordshire Pottery. Even quite small backyard potters sometimes mixed their own clay body and jealously guarded its secrets from their rivals, while others bought from their larger neighbours. The potter's merchant, supplying clay and other materials from a centralized source, did not appear until quite late in the century, round about 1870. Much confusion has been caused by these facts never having been made sufficiently clear to Victorian Staffordshire collectors.

From the eighteenth century to the beginning of our period was a time of ceaseless experiment to produce bodies with finer, more sophisticated characteristics than those yielded by the local clays. Before the days of accurate chemical analysis this caused endless difficulties and frustrations. Impurities in natural clay and mineral deposits used in these experiments could vary within yards, giving rise to bodies having marked differences when they left the oven. Even small traces of iron, for instance, would cause the clay to take on a yellow or brownish tinge after firing.

43. Admiral Blake. c.1851. 10 in.

44. Florence Nightingale by Sampson Smith. Very lightweight earthenware. c.1856 and later. $14\frac{1}{2}$ in.

Only two small deposits in North Staffordshire yielded good white clay. It was for this reason that the Staffordshire potters began using clays from Cornwall including the fine white china clay and china stone. These last were stable in quality and had few impurities.

Their introduction to the Potteries was complicated because, as we have seen, they were also essential ingredients of porcelain. Their use in the manufacture of pottery was restricted by law until Wedgwood was instrumental in securing their release in 1755. His taste may be questionable, but his industry was tremendous. His experiments with many different natural minerals, not only from England but from China and America, helped to establish Staffordshire as one of the greatest ceramic centres of the world. When he wasn't busy icing his cakes he was promoting canals and agitating for new and better turnpike roads to replace the rutted cart tracks of his day. Easier transportation made sure that not only his own products, but those of even the humblest back-street potters in the Victorian age, could be sold economically in every corner of the land. There was a large export trade to Europe and America but, with few exceptions, our figures were obviously aimed at the home market (see also Chapter 5).

33

To delve too deeply into the precise chemical composition of these different ceramic bodies is to invite madness, and for the average collector it is unnecessary. But it is important for him to realize that the body of Victorian figures varied a great deal from earthenware to porcelain with numerous permutations in between, and also that a figure will vary in weight and translucency according to the composition of its body. This is one reason why the subject is more complicated than has generally been realized.

I am not suggesting that a back-street potter could nip up to one of his grander neighbours and pinch his secret formulas. What I do say is that by the time our figures were made the experiments of the eighteenth-century and early nineteenth-century master potters had a direct result on the products of even the smallest Victorian pot-bank. Workmen moved from place to place and no secret was safe for ever. The danger for a new collector is that he tends to assume that the quality of this heterogeneous output remained constant. 'Staffordshire Pottery is Staffordshire Pottery,' he says; and obviously nothing could be farther from the truth. Quality varied enormously. Why not? We are not examining the tidy documented output of a single large factory, but the unrecorded products of an area some thirty square miles in extent; an area turning out figures in different bodies and in qualities ranging from bad to superb. There are rare figures, common figures, figures you get sick of seeing, and figures you have never seen before. This huge happy ceramic explosion of untutored art has all been lumped together and dubbed Staffordshire Pottery. The term will probably always be with us and it doesn't matter as long as we, as collectors, understand what it means and learn to judge each figure on its merits.

Nearly a fifth of the figures in my own collection have some porcellaneous qualities. For our purpose this is only a grander way of saying that if you get your eye really close to that little vent hole in the base or the back of the figure, and then hold it close to a strong electric bulb, you may find that it transmits a little (or quite a lot of) light. I am too lazy to check all the figures in the shop, but looking around the shelves, I think a fifth again is a very fair estimate. These porcellaneous figures are invariably well potted, of good quality and always worth looking for. At the time of writing they are undervalued and underpriced. It may be noticed that I have confined this chapter to a discussion of the body of the figure. I have done this deliberately, because I believe it to be important and neglected. Glaze, decoration and colour we can deal with later as we come to them.

It is interesting to note that the potters themselves divided their products quite firmly into two main categories of earthenware and chinaware and it is not clear where they drew the dividing line. We may see from reading *The Ceramic Art of Great Britain* by Llewellynn Jewitt published in 1878 that the output of the factories both large and small varied considerably, both in the range of goods produced

45. Crimean naval gunners by Thomas Parr. *c*.1855. 10 in.   46. Louis Kossuth. Hungarian patriot. *c*.1851. 10¾ in.

and in the materials with which they were made. Two entries under Hanley are listed as follows:

William Stubbs, Eastwood Pottery, manufactures china and earthenware services of the commoner kinds, lustres, stoneware jugs, black teapots, etc. and the smaller and commoner classes of china toys and ornaments. [Toys, images and chimney ornaments were all words used to describe our figures.]

Percy Street, William Machin, makes ordinary earthenware and common coloured figures.

Other contemporary accounts of the Potteries refer to both earthenware- and china-manufacturers, making it clear that some of them produced both. In 1900 an old potter recalled his early life as a child labourer aged seven in such a place (*When I was a Child* by an old Potter [C. Shaw]). He had been making handles for earthenware cups and says, 'It came about that after one of the box-rope floggings by the drunken "handler" for whom I worked I was sent to work at the lower bank where chinaware was manufactured'. The *Report of the Royal Commission on Children's Employment in Industry* in 1843 is particular in placing even small factories into

35

47. Admirals Sir Charles Napier and Sir James Deans Dundas. Crimean War. These figures are known to differ in height, weight, modelling, decoration, factory and title, Admiral Napier (on the left) having also been seen titled Sir E. Lyons and Admiral Dundas. This new source (48) helps to explain why. *c.*1854. 16 in. 15½ in.

48. Admirals Sir E. Lyons, Sir Charles Napier, and Sir James Deans Dundas. *Cassells Illustrated Family Paper*, 7 October 1854.

one category or another, or stating that they made both. It seems possible and likely that certain figures were made in both sections of the same factory, and at the same time.

The praying figure of "Madame Vestris as Paul" (8) also appears in earthenware with more solid modelling (49) and, for obvious commercial reasons, the two figures are likely to be contemporary. There is a theory that the earthenware figure was produced later, possibly when Vestris died in 1856, but I think this unlikely. (See chapter 1 page 6.) Our Victorian figures, then, can be either heavy or quite light in weight, completely opaque, very slightly translucent, or of porcelain, which transmits a lot of light. All of them could well have been made within a few hundred yards of each other and at the same period of time. A collector who knows that these variations can be contemporary will not be nearly so confused as I was when I first started to collect. When I think back to some of the things I was told by some dealers who should have known better, I blush for them even now. A porcelain or semi-porcelain figure was invariably called 'Rockingham'. Indeed sometimes it didn't even have to be porcellaneous; many a good solid earthenware

Prince Alfred. *c.*1858. 10¾ in.   Colour Plate 2.

49. Earthenware figure of Madame Vestris.
Date doubtful. 7 in.
In the collection of Surgeon Captain
P. D. G. Pugh.

figure decorated with blobs of clay sausaged through a fine wire sieve was given the same attribution. The myth of the ubiquitous Rockingham figure dies hard. Even today collectors will often find unmarked Victorian Staffordshire porcelain figures of good quality being offered for sale as Rockingham. Less understandably, collectors of some experience still persist in thinking that some of their figures are Rockingham, an entrenched attitude which modern research and two authoritative books on the factory and its products have done little to change.

These are the facts. The Rockingham factory produced porcelain only for the short period of sixteen years from 1826 to its closure in 1842. Furthermore, there is strong evidence to suggest that their figures were made for an even shorter period, from 1826 to 1830, and that all such figures would bear the following marks impressed beneath a simple solid base: the Rockingham Griffin and/or ROCK-INGHAM WORKS BRAMELD, together with an incised mould number from 1 to 120. If the figure is very small it may only carry the mould number and an unidentified code CI of 1, 2, 3, 4, etc., up to 15. If the figure does not conform to these standards, it will almost certainly be Staffordshire porcelain and has every right to be judged as that on its own merits, for some of them are very fine indeed. Such figures are often dated arbitrarily by the composition of their bodies. They are given an earlier date, sometimes as much as twenty years before the earthenware version, which is inaccurate and confusing. Certainly it *could* happen (some sub-

50. Collection of Staffordshire cottages and castles some often wrongly called Rockingham. In a private collection.

jects remained popular for many years) but to lay it down as a fixed rule is not supported by the facts.

Weight and body, then, are not accurate guides to date, and a new collector ought not to let anyone blind him with science. Later, with experience, the body of a figure might suggest certain possibilities, but as a factor taken in isolation it is of less significance than subject, decoration and palette. Whatever the particular composition of its clay, the figure was moulded from an original model and given its first firing to emerge from the potter's oven in the state known as 'biscuit'. Subsequent processes decorated it and covered it with a thin film of glass, which was of course the final glaze. I have deliberately condensed all that information in the last two sentences because we have had quite enough technicalities for this chapter. Later we can spread ourselves, and follow these stages in more detail at leisure to arrive at our finished figure. Meanwhile I see no reason why we shouldn't jump ahead and look at a splendid example of a Victorian Staffordshire figure at its best.

The colour plate 2 shows a figure of Queen Victoria's second son Prince Alfred, born 6 August 1844. It was most probably made in 1858, the year he received his first commission as a naval cadet to commemorate his maiden voyage on H.M.S. *Euryalus*. His father, Prince Albert, insisted that his son's uniform should be no different from his fellow cadets', and Queen Victoria had it sent to her in London, just to make sure. It was, after all, at that time the most famous uniform in the world, and aroused deep feelings in the heart of every Englishman – in other words, a best-seller. The little fourteen-year-old boy was seen safely on board by a doting father and his elder brother the Prince of Wales. Bands played, flags waved, and 'the magnificent new steam-assisted frigate' sailed proudly from Spithead on Wednesday, 27 October 1858.

The body is white earthenware and obviously one of the first out of the mould, beautifully sharp and fine, with every detail clean and crisp. The painting of the face and waistcoat shows every sign that great care was taken with the decoration – no rush job this. The underglaze cobalt blue is deep and lustrous, the overglaze enamel colours are fresh and evenly applied and they have not flaked. All the detail is superb. Look at the sharpness of the rope, the plaited straw of his hat, and the features of the face with eyes detailed in the mould itself. In fact many of the details which in a lesser figure would have been merely painted on in enamel colours are here found in the mould: his sash and Order, his belt buckle, even his waistcoat pocket. Take a closer look at the decoration. There are over a hundred and thirty brush strokes on the waistcoat, and each hair of his eyebrows is painted separately. The general condition is excellent, there is no damage or restoration. His head and his vulnerable hat have both survived intact, and his nose is not chipped or scuffed. Some of the gilt on the raised capitals of his name is a little rubbed, as it is on his jacket, but it's not too bad, and we are after all judging a near-perfect figure by extreme standards.

Everything about it gladdens the eye of the collector and dealer alike. Not one of the really rare figures, but one to add colour and charm to any collection. But forget all the details which add up to make this particular figure a good specimen (from more than three feet away you couldn't see most of them anyway). Just stand back and look at the figure itself. It has a simplicity and uncomplicated vigour which sing out and hold the eye clear across the room. It has an economy of line which fifty years later was to be hailed as new in the works of Picasso and Rousseau.

While the sophisticated potters were busy importing foreign designers and modellers, like Arnoux, Carrier, Meli and Solon, and sinking deeper and deeper into yet another Classical revival, while the Great Exhibition and the 'Art Union of London' were fostering yet more examples of what Jewitt called 'the highest achievements of ceramic art', small back-street hovels a stone's throw away were making figures like this with a native simplicity which owed nothing to any foreign influence. Jewitt's 'common coloured figures' are as English as Staffordshire itself, but the Staffordshire of pubs and Primitive Methodism and premature death, not the Staffordshire of Solon and Etruria and Elysium. The wonder is, not the high prices which some of them fetch at auction, but that they have been ignored for so long.

❧ 4 ❧
How They were Made

We have seen how the style developed, and we can now understand perhaps a little more clearly the great variations in the material of which they were made. There is no great mystery about the method of their manufacture. We can, and will, follow the process slowly because this is the best way for a collector to be able to assess, as he must, the merits of each individual figure. There is no other way to judge Victorian Staffordshire for there is a great variation in quality.

The figures from the big, well-documented factories, both in the Potteries and elsewhere, present in comparison far fewer problems for the collector. Records were kept, and diligent patient researchers can trace with a fair degree of accuracy the work of certain modellers and decorators. 'Look,' they say. 'Here is the work of such and such a man, the factory records show that he was a modeller at the time. He was born here, and worked there, and died and was buried in this or that churchyard, and this is what he made.' Fine – we may envy them their tidy records, and be grateful for the added knowledge and interest they bring, but such luxuries are not for us. Staffordshire is not a well-documented factory. It is native primitive art, cheerfully blowing away the more pretentious turgidities of its grander contemporaries like a great breath of fresh air. It has been unsung and underestimated for far too many years. As we have seen, many of the figures were made in anonymous pot-banks in conditions of squalor, brutality, semi-starvation, disease and vice – if you can call a little fornication vice. The ladies who worked in the throwing room were generally acknowledged to be the most kind-hearted – but we digress.

51. Grinding and preparing the various colours for the Enameller or Painter.

52. First process of potting is "Throwing", forming round pieces of ware with the Hands and Machine.

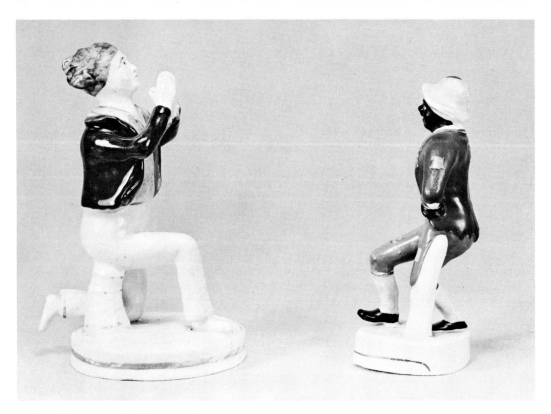

53. Pre-Victorian style of figure. *c.*1822.
6¾ in. *c.*1836. 5¾ in.

Many of these small pot-banks kept no detailed records, they had no such desire,
and if they had they were prevented from doing so because often their owners
couldn't write. Sometimes the master of such a place had risen from the bench
himself, and was as illiterate as the workers he employed. The term 'folk art' has
become debased, with its overtones of petrified pixie pottery from Polperro, but in
the sense of meaning art made for common people by common people, that is
exactly what our figures are – the last great folk art made in England.

Just as few detailed records of our potters survive, so it is not surprising to find
that they very rarely used a factory mark. The names of many of them have been
recorded from various sources, but the difficulties of ascribing figures to a particular
potter with accuracy are almost insurmountable, nor do I believe it to be of the
first importance. At the beginning it is surely better for a collector not to confuse
himself with hundreds of names laboriously culled from rate books, old histories,
and wills. When he has been at it for some years, and knows instinctively when
something is 'right' or 'wrong', then he can consider the possible attributions to
his heart's content and derive great pleasure from it, but to begin with it can be
more confusing than helpful. Balston wisely confined himself to the broadest of

54. Style of modelling. *c.*1830–40.

55. This illustration and 56 show how the figures began to develop into the 'flat-back' style. They were all made in the 1840s.

56. Style of modelling. *c.*1845.

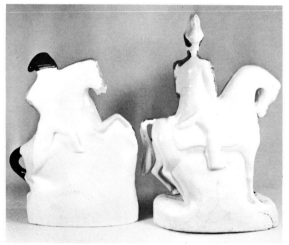

57. 'Flat back' figures. *c.*1850–56. Many others were completely flat-backed.

classifications, and for convenience' sake was content to group together figures bearing similar characteristics and to suggest factory names for them. A thoroughly sound simplification at the time he was writing and one which has served collectors very well until now. (See also chapters 5 and 8.)

Changes in style of Victorian Staffordshire figures present no great problems for the collector. The pre-Victorian style of figures like Vestris and Rice (53,) modelled in the round, sometimes with a short supporting column, gave way in the 1840s to a simple oval or scroll base with the figure still modelled in the round above it. From this point to the end of the century, with few exceptions, the style deve-

58. Sancho Panza and Don Quixote. Made by Thomas Parr. *c*.1855. 8 in. 9¾ in.

loped slowly, and the following changes occurred. Modelling in the round was gradually abandoned, until the figures were almost completely flat-backed and designed to be viewed from the front only. No doubt it was their popularity as chimney ornaments on the mantel-shelf which influenced the potters. The flat-back figure was cheaper to make, and we as collectors gain by the enforced simplicity of design.

It is interesting to look at the backs of some flat-back figures which still have some details moulded on them, almost as though the modeller could not quite persuade himself to abandon his previous style (57). In the 1840s and '50s figures were mostly lavishly coloured with cobalt blue and bright enamels and rich gilding. For the rest of the period the colouring gradually became more subdued, although the use of cobalt blue continued for longer than has been thought. Different potters varied in style and use of colour of course – the Tallis-type figures are an extreme example (58) – but on the whole the development was even and gradual.

It is surely better to consider the anonymous output of Staffordshire as a conglomerate whole and to assess merit on single pieces instead of by dubious attributions to individual potters, however fascinating the pursuit.

I am perfectly happy to spend days in museums and libraries, trying to establish one small extra piece of evidence that may or may not put a figure in a particular

44

potter's back yard. Our concern here, however, is less ambitious: only to recognize a good figure and to know why it is good, and to suggest some new ideas for collectors to consider.

Most of a collector's experience and knowledge will come through actually handling the figure himself, and by talking to other collectors and dealers. I have never understood why some dealers are reluctant to pass on their knowledge to collectors. They are very much a minority but it seems daft to me. The more interested and more knowledgeable a collector becomes through a dealer's help and advice, the more likely he is to trust him and accept his guidance. When I first began to collect it was not from books that I learned, but from a handful of devoted dealers who helped and encouraged me. To them I shall always be grateful. All my best pieces I bought when I trusted them before I had learned to avoid expensive mistakes, and I have never had cause to regret that trust.

Museums are a great help, although even today Victorian Staffordshire figures are very much neglected as far as most museums are concerned. When they are given a little space a collector should go and see them even if he can't handle them. If the staff are not too busy, it's always worth asking if they will let you see anything they have which is not on display. I have found figures tucked away in museum basements that turned me green with envy.

When factory-marked pieces do turn up they are rare and always command high prices, out of all proportion to unmarked pieces of higher quality. The figure itself is much more important than the mark, but not many people believe it. In a way we are lucky that it is so; we are exempt from that well-known collector's disease of Mark Mania, and must learn to use our eyes, rather than a set of listed labels. No factory mark ever turned a poor figure into a good one and for us their interest is historical rather than an indication of merit. Having said that, I must admit I wish I had some factory marks in my own private collection, but I haven't, so perhaps sour grapes comes into it a bit. Let's just say that a *high quality* figure bearing the name of the factory is very desirable, but they are rare enough not to trouble a beginner. Occasionally an unmarked figure will share so many identical characteristics with a figure which bears a factory mark that it may be identified with confidence as a product of that same factory and probably from the hand of the same modeller (see colour plate 3).

We should be grateful to those researchers who have so painstakingly compiled lists of marks with such patience and accuracy, but for Staffordshire figures you need more than a mark, you need an eye, and for that you need help. No book can be a substitute for experience, but it should help to cut one or two corners, and to point out some nasty traps for the unwary. Later we can examine fakes, forgeries and reproductions, but before we can see why a figure is 'wrong' we must follow the original process of manufacture and see what makes it 'right'.

45

59. The Modeller or Sculptor from whose productions are taken casts or moulds for the potter.

For us, as collectors, probably the most interesting man in the pot-bank is the modeller, the man responsible for the original figure, made free-hand in an oily clay from which the mould was made. The sources of his inspiration are discussed later but for the moment let us consider what happened to that original model. In the simplest terms, a plaster-of-Paris mould was taken of it, and eventually from this mould came the clay figure (whatever its composition might be) which was then fired in the first oven, emerging in the biscuit state to be decorated and glazed. I say eventually, because figures were seldom made direct from that first mould. As the original clay model was spoiled in the first moulding it was obviously prudent to retain a replica of it. This was done by making the first impression from that mould not in clay but in plaster-of-Paris. So now we have a spoiled original clay model which was discarded, but we also have a perfect replica of it in plaster-of-Paris, carefully stored in case an accident destroyed or damaged the mould. As a further safeguard, not only was the plaster figure of the original model preserved, but a master mould of it, also in plaster, was taken and kept safe. From this master mould any number of plaster moulds (known as working moulds) could be made. If the figure proved popular this was necessary, for a working mould could only be used for a limited number of times before it became worn, thus producing inferior figures lacking in sharp definition.

Now the information in that last paragraph is important for collectors, for we can now see why a good sharp figure need not necessarily be earlier than a blurred

46

60. Fairground or Astley dancer. *c*.1855. 9½ in.

61. Unidentified theatre or fairground musicians. *c*.1855. 7¾ in.

62. Most likely to be George Parr, captain of the All England XI (1857–70) and Julius Caesar, famous batsman All England XI (1849–67). *c*.1865. 14 in.

63. Sailor and girl; probably Crimean period. *c*.1854. 11¼ in.

figure, because it could well have come from a new working mould. I had considered a diagram to illustrate all this but whenever I see a diagram in a book my heart sinks, however clear it may be.

Let us consider the simplest figure of all, one made from a two-piece mould, each piece containing the impression of half the figure, front and back. A 'bat' of body clay, like pastry, was pressed firmly into each half of the mould and the surplus neatly trimmed flush with a knife. These trimmed edges were then brushed over with liquid clay (or slip), and the two halves of the mould bound tightly together with cord. Now you could still have access to the inside of the figure through the open bottom of the mould, and thin rolls of clay body could be pressed well into the seams to ensure a good join. If you are ever unfortunate enough to break a figure you will be able to see the finger-prints of the workman quite easily. So in fact every figure carries its own secret factory mark locked away inside. A splendid unexplored field for research, waiting only for a retired fingerprint expert with a collection of broken figures.

The dry porous plaster now absorbed some of the water in the clay, and the mould was placed in a heated room to accelerate this process. After a period of time the figure shrank and could easily be removed from the mould. It was further dried to a leather-hard state, and could then be handled and stood upright without danger of distortion. In this condition it was still possible to cover up any obvious faults (perhaps caused by an air bubble) and smooth away any seam marks. At this point too, the open bottom of the figure was usually sealed with a slightly concave base made from a one-piece mould to fit exactly and stuck on with slip. This simple figure was now ready for its first firing (60, 61, 62 and 63)

If however the figure was more complicated, as many of them were, with separate arms and legs, or anything which would have prevented the figure from being extracted clean from the mould without being broken, these extra bits would have been made in separate moulds and stuck on to the figure with slip at this stage. The joins were then smoothed and trimmed and tidied as before by a man known as a repairer. Sometimes it was possible to avoid the extra work involved with these subsidiary parts. For example, the space between an arm with hand on hip and the body could be cut out when the clay was still leather-hard, but many figures did have extra bits stuck on. Now too were added those little clumps of grasslike decoration made by squeezing clay through a fine wire sieve, thus providing some future dealers with an instant 'Rockingham' figure (64, 65 and 66). Small holes were made in the figure to allow the expanding air to escape in the firing, sometimes in the base, but often behind if the figure was a flat-back; a large figure might have both. A figure like a spill vase incorporating a natural opening would not need any. Figures with large, neat, perfectly circular holes in the base as big as a halfpenny (or whatever the horrid decimal equivalent may be) are always very

64. Lady Sale. Her husband, Sir Robert Sale, commanded the fort at Jalalabad in 1842. She took part in the terrifying British retreat from Kabul, was shot through the arm and a prisoner of the Afghans for seven months. Her *Journal of the Disasters in Afghanistan* was published in 1843; this is, therefore, the earliest dateable non-royal titled Staffordshire figure. (Pair to Sir Robert Sale.) *c.*1843. 7¼ in.

late, if not modern. As this book may be read in years to come, it may be helpful to state that the diameter of an old halfpenny was exactly one inch. If inches have given way to centimetres then I refuse to help you further, and you must work it out for yourself.

These stages we have just been looking at can again help the collector. Once a figure had received its first firing no further tidying or correction of faults could be done. Apart from decoration the figure was virtually complete, and any careless or slip-shod work from the repairer was set for ever.

There was a variation in the process of moulding, a 'slip' or 'cast' mould being very occasionally used. The empty mould was tied together and filled with liquid slip; after a short time the porous plaster of the mould absorbed the water from the slip nearest to it, forming a layer of clay body. The rest of the liquid slip was then poured away and when the remaining clay became firm enough to handle or leather-hard the figure could be removed from the mould as before. The base of

49

65. Duke of Wellington on Copenhagen at Waterloo. One of the most sought after figures and very difficult to find; even later reproductions are rare now. Made by Thomas Parr. $c.$1860. $11\frac{1}{2}$ in.

66. Elizabeth Barrett Browning and Flush.
c.1846. 5¼ in.

these figures, which are often porcellaneous, was sometimes, but not always, left open.

The figure, now complete apart from colouring and glaze, was given its first and hottest firing in the biscuit oven at about 1100 degrees centigrade, emerging hard, stable, brittle and porous.

Colour was added to the figure in two ways, under the glaze or above it. Colour under the glaze had to be capable of standing up to the firing heat of the glaze or glost oven without changing, and only two colours which could pass this test were used for our figures. The one which is almost a trade mark for Victorian Staffordshire is of course the famous cobalt blue (see Chapter 1 page 8), but a good deep black could be made by mixing cobalt oxide with manganese and iron oxides. It is possible for an earthenware figure to have a lower glost oven firing temperature, thus allowing the use of other underglaze colours produced by the oxides of copper, antimony, chrome and tin. The higher glost oven temperature necessary for porcelain prohibits the use of all underglaze colours except black and cobalt blue and in practice these are the only two colours found under the glaze of our Victorian Staffordshire figures, whether the body is of earthenware or porcelain.

Balston says that underglaze black was rarely used, listing only some twenty odd figures by name. In practice, through the years, I have found it used fairly freely, even though on balance the duller overglaze black is more common. It should not be thought that a figure with underglaze black is necessarily to be preferred to the

51

68. Highwaymen Tom King and Dick Turpin; underglaze black horses, enamel black hair. Theatrical, probably Astley's. *c.*1847. 9 in.

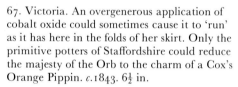

67. Victoria. An overgenerous application of cobalt oxide could sometimes cause it to 'run' as it has here in the folds of her skirt. Only the primitive potters of Staffordshire could reduce the majesty of the Orb to the charm of a Cox's Orange Pippin. *c.*1843. 6½ in.

one that has enamel black. For some strange reason quite a few figures turn up with both, underglaze boots perhaps, and enamel hats. The choice seems to have been quite arbitrary, and I can only think that the working conditions must have been responsible for it (68).

These two underglaze colours were painted on the biscuit figure with turpentine or a fat oil medium and given a light firing in the oven at about 650 degrees centigrade to set them, the object being to stop them dissolving in the liquid glaze when the figure was dipped and contaminating it with their strong colour. The figure with its fixed underglaze colours was now dipped by hand into a vat of liquid lead glaze which became a thin film of glass when the figure was fired in the glost oven at over 900 degrees centigrade. Most of our figures have a good generous coating of glaze, and where it forms a slightly thicker layer in pockets and crevices of the moulding, it is often tinged with blue.

A far greater range of colours could be used if they were painted on after the figure had been glazed, including the gold or gilt decoration. These enamel colours were metallic oxides and were blended with a special flux which became hard and

69. The murder of Thomas Smith by William Collier at Kingsley, Staffordshire in 1866. Collier was hanged on 7 August 1866, the last execution in public at Stafford Gaol. It was an inexpert job, the rope knot slipped and the wretched Collier was led up from the pit to be hanged again. Left to right: (a) enamel colours, (b) white and gilt, (c) underglaze cobalt blue and enamel colours. *c.*1866. 13½ in.

glass-like at fairly low temperatures, round about 800 degrees centigrade. At this temperature the glaze would usually soften enough to fuse with the metallic oxides and the flux and hold them firm, and their colour remained true. The advantage of enamel overglaze colours is a far wider range of palette. The disadvantage is that if applied too thickly they tend to flake off in patches, leaving the glazed white surface of the figure exposed. They sometimes have a rather dull matt surface, although at their best they look magnificent with a good surface shine almost equal to the underglaze colours. Pink was particularly good in this respect and at first sight often appears to be under the glaze, but it is an overglaze enamel. It is worth noting that the choice of colours, both under and over the glaze, seems to have been purely arbitrary. Figures, otherwise identical, have been found with various combinations of colour (69); these have no significance.

Gold decoration was used on the figures right through from the early pre-Victorian figures (8) up to the end of the century. Balston says that 'mercuric

70. 'Aqua Regia' gold title. *c.*1864. 5 in.

gold' was used, that is, an amalgam of gold and mercury with flux, but in fact this formula was very rarely used in Staffordshire because it was highly toxic. The potters were even more afraid of mercury than they were of lead (see Chapter 2) and almost all our figures were gilded by the 'aqua regia gold' process. Gold filings were dissolved in aqua regia. After drying, the resultant finely divided gold powder was mixed and applied with a borax flux and fired. This produced a splendid, soft, gently glowing gold. The later 'liquid gold' is harsh and brassy compared with the earlier gold. Balston also says that this liquid gold was first introduced in the early 1880s, but in fact the first recorded use of it was as early as 1858. Some good figures have been unfairly given a later date because of this error, and it's worth remembering that because a figure has bright liquid gold it is by no means certain to be as late as Balston would suggest. Both forms are liable to rub off, especially when painted over raised surfaces like titles and medals, and even on flat surfaces. Gold decoration is discussed further in Chapter 8. After this final firing to soften and fix the enamel colours and the gilt, the figure was complete.

These technicalities are important, because they help a collector to see the finer points of a piece he may buy, and later to see the difference between an original figure and a reproduction. But enough is enough. Have a rest and look at "The Victory" (colour plate 4). Now there's a good old flag-waving bit of nonsense for you. That should cheer you up, and it makes all the points discussed in this chapter. The only underglaze colour is the cobalt blue of the Turkish soldier's jacket; all the

71. 'The Real Peace Negotiators'. *Cassell's Illustrated Family Paper*, 15 March 1856. Newly discovered source of Colour Plate 4. "The Victory".

rest are overglaze enamel and you can see what a variety of colour they made possible. At first sight the pink at the top of the right-hand flag appears to be under-glaze, but it is in fact a well-fused overglaze enamel. The black enamel has flaked a bit, and black seems to be particularly inclined to do this. The gold is subdued and glowing and not too badly rubbed. The lead glaze is generous and soft, showing blue tints where it lies trapped and thickest. The best place to see this is in the folds of the sailor's trousers.

At first sight you might think that some subsidiary moulds were used, but not a bit of it. That is from a perfectly simple two-piece mould, and an excellent example of the Victorian potter's ingenuity, and ability to condense his subject and dispense with unnecessary detail. That he was forced into simplicity of line by the economics of the potting is our good fortune and does nothing to detract from his achievement. It's interesting too look at his probable source of inspiration (71) and see what he made of it. Just think of the possible complications, neatly avoided, and consider what one of his grander neighbours might have turned out.

And there it is – a real bit of tub-thumping 'Rule Britannia', like a brass band on a sunny day with the British Tar in pride of place above France and Turkey, who were lucky enough to be allowed to share his victory, even if they didn't get a drink. Uncomplicated native art, made at a time when some sophisticated English factories were still wearily plodding after Dresden and Sèvres, and busy churning out dreary derivative ladies with the ultimate horror of imitation lace knickers. Such factories claimed to be superior to the French which is, after all, exactly what our British sailor thought, only he says it better. The figure commemorates the victory of the Allied Powers over Russia in the Crimea in 1856. The potter's victory has taken longer to establish.

5

Identification (Part 1)

There are two main ways of identifying an unnamed figure. One is by finding a print which has obviously inspired the modeller, and the other by a method I have evolved for myself over the years when no print can be found. The first method is sometimes, but not always, more conclusive, and the second I shall describe in the next chapter.

Some years ago Messrs Mander and Mitchenson, the theatre historians, found that a series of figures bearing common characteristics was in fact closely copied from illustrations engraved in a publication called *Tallis' Shakespeare Gallery* (1852–3). It was this discovery that caused Balston to invent the name 'Tallis Factory' and, for convenience' sake, to attribute to it all figures bearing certain characteristics of modelling, palette and body.

These so-called 'Tallis' figures are always modelled in the round and painted with enamel colours only; there are no underglaze colours. They are made of a good solid heavy earthenware body and some are titled or carry quotations in transfer printing, others are untitled, and a third category has the title in indented capital letters. The bases are painted with long brush strokes in pastel shades of green, yellow and brown. In later versions, however, some bases remained unpainted. These 'Tallis' figures are not typcial and owe more to the tradition of porcelain than earthenware. In a way are the odd man out of the usual, more primitive range of Staffordshire figures. Some of them, especially the equestrian figures, are superbly modelled and would make an impressive collection (72, 73 and 65).

On the whole 'Tallis Factory' has been a very useful shorthand method of indicating a type of potting, but it has its dangers, for much later figures made by several other potters display almost identical characteristics. (See also Chapter 8.)

Balston's so-called 'Alpha Factory' figures are also well modelled, but although the body is more porcellaneous they are nearer to the spirit of the true Staffordshire tradition. They have both underglaze and enamel colours and are sometimes titled with indented capital letters or occasionally with gilt cursive script. They are often quite complicated, requiring several subsidiary moulds. Many small factories probably made figures with similar characteristics and the use of the term 'Alpha Factory' could store up confusion in the future. A selection of this type of figure is shown in 74–9. 'Alpha' is a good useful word but 'Alpha-type' is more accurate than 'Alpha Factory'.

57

73. Probably a portrait of Lady Hester Stanhope. *c*.1852. 9 in.

72. Omar Pasha. Turkish general, Crimean War. Made by Thomas Parr. *c*.1854. 10¾ in.

The significant discovery was Mander & Mitchenson's, for it suggested very strongly that if a modeller could use illustrations from Tallis, there was no reason why other illustrations could not have been used in the same way, and this has proved to be the case. Scrivens records an interview with a modeller in his report (from which I have already quoted in Chapter 2).

Edward Key was forty-four and had worked as a potter for thirty-three years. He worked with one other modeller in a small room. He said:

'My duty is to make models to pattern, from drawings, sometimes from taste; they go from me to the mould makers upstairs.'

He thought the work healthy and was paid by the piece.

Now although Key did not work for one of the smaller pot-banks, his evidence is interesting and suggests the method of modellers in Staffordshire at that time (circa 1840) and throughout the century. The difficulty is, of course, to find the original print. A page-by-page scrutiny of every book, magazine or newspaper illustrated in the nineteenth century would undoubtedly clear up many unsolved mysteries but is regrettably impossible.

The field can be narrowed to more manageable proportions in two ways. One is

74. Mrs Amelia Bloomer's famous costume. c.1851. 9½ in.

75. Jenny Lind as Marie in Donizetti's *Daughter of the Regiment*. Act I. c.1848. 8 in.

76. Jenny Lind; same opera, quick change for Act II. c.1848. 7¾ in.

77. Eliza Cook wrote really appallingly bad poems, some of them dedicated to the American actress Charlotte Cushman (218). c.1849. 10¾ in.

78. Byron. c.1848. 7½ in.

79. Probably Eliza Cook and Byron or the Brownings. c.1846. 6¾ in.

80. Cricketers Fuller
Pilch and Thomas
Box. *c*. 1843. $7\frac{1}{2}$ in.
$6\frac{1}{2}$ in. In the collec-
tion of Mr I. N. R.
Shield.
Photograph by
courtesy of Surgeon
Captain P. D. G.
Pugh.

PORTRAIT OF PILCH.

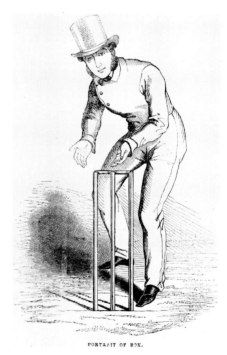

PORTRAIT OF BOX.

81. *Illustrated London News*, 15 July 1843.

to comb the sources already known to have been used by the potters. It is a slow, plodding job but I have found it fascinating and rewarding. The other sounds more formidable but it isn't really. It consists of immersing oneself in the history of the Victorian age and trying to see the world through the eyes of a working potter of those days. That is why the earlier chapters of this book are designed to help and encourage a collector if part of his pleasure is to come from research and the identification of anonymous figures he may be curious about. It depends on the individual. If a collector wants to sit back and admire his figures and let them appreciate in value, why not? He needn't stir a finger; the chances are that someone will do the research for him sooner or later anyway.

If we remember that the first priority of every potter, large or small, was to make money, the field again narrows considerably. Given his loyalty, his patriotism, his strong Methodist beliefs, and his support and need for radical reform, his viewpoint becomes clearer still. National events that caught the attention of the newspapers were likely to be exactly the same things which the potter felt might be modelled and sold to advantage. A national hero might die, or write his autobiography, and biographies were sometimes illustrated. Heroes and events were of course suitably filtered through his strong left-wing bias. Revolutionaries of his own or other countries were much in favour. Yet a rough order of precedence, in a potter's eyes, would seem to be: Napoleon Bonaparte, Queen Victoria, John Wesley, the British Sailor, generals and admirals (whatever their politics), actors, revolutionaries, sportsmen, murderers, Jesus Christ and Poets (preferably left-wing of course). The only truly right-wing politician who was recorded by them was Disraeli, who was beloved by the Queen and added several million square miles to her Empire (really a general could hardly have done as much) and he made a convenient pair to Gladstone.

By 1842 *The Illustrated London News* was being sold containing many wood engravings, and the first of these to catch the potter's eye were the cricketers Fuller Pilch and Thomas Box (80), from the July issue of 1843, page 45 (81). No one needed to tell the potters that cricket was popular in England and their early choice of these illustrations is a fair indication of the way their minds were working. To confound my order of precedence they were intrigued by a crusading Roman Catholic priest, Father Mathew, (82, 193) inspired by the story and drawings in the issue of July 1843, page 853. But then Father Mathew was news, and news sold figures. He deserves more space later. (See Chapter 7, pages 127–9.)

It has been accepted until now that when an illustration was used as a source, then it would be reproduced as accurately as possible, with great fidelity and with great attention to detail. This does the potters less than justice. The truth is that some modellers did indeed do this, but that others adapted and made alterations to suit themselves. There was too the question of simplifying the design to make the

82. Father Theobald Mathew.
c.1843. 6¾ in. In the collection of
Surgeon Captain P. D. G. Pugh.

potting easier. The modeller who copied Nathaniel Dance's portrait of Captain Cook (83) has given us a highly accurate version of it, but not without some difficulty, for to complete his figure required no less than eight separate moulds (84). This explains why such extreme accuracy was not always attempted. We are lucky that it was so for, as we have seen in "The Victory" (colour plate 4), it was the economics of potting that forced them into simplicity and so gave us figures of such power and vigour which are only now being appreciated at their true value. (In a similar way the B.B.C. has produced film documentaries of genius on a shoe string, while one prefers to forget more pretentious efforts made with the millions of Hollywood behind them.)

Cassell's Illustrated Family Paper had not been discovered as a source until I was lucky enough to unearth some copies in the basement of the London Library, and it was here that I found the source of "The Victory". It is interesting to see the different approach of the modeller to another figure taken from this newspaper. "The Wounded Soldier" (85 and 86) required less adaptation than "The Victory" and the modeller was clever enough to recognize this. He saw at once the drama of

83. Captain James Cook. Oil painting by Nathaniel
Dance, 1776. By courtesy of the National Maritime
Museum, Greenwich.

84. Captain James Cook, explorer extraordinary.
c.1847. $7\frac{1}{2}$ in.

the two central figures of the soldier and the sailor, and realized that with very little
alteration it could be made in a simple mould. He was content to let it speak for
itself – the simplicity was already there. With the Crimean War occupying the
thoughts of the whole country, and with all the publicity which had been given to
the suffering of the wounded, he must have known he was on to a good thing.

This print as a source is doubly interesting for it provides a possible answer to a
problem which had puzzled me for some years. The figure (87) titled "Sailor
Return" in gilt script is the only recorded example so titled. When it first came into
the shop neither my partner nor I could think why its original identity had been
changed. Usually it is titled in gilt script, "George and Eliza Harris", two characters in *Uncle Tom's Cabin* by Harriet Beecher Stowe (1811–96). The book, published
in 1852, made a tremendous impression in England and was dramatized many
times, notably in a three-act version by E. Fitzball called *Uncle Tom's Cabin; or
The Horrors of Slavery* at Drury Lane in December 1852.

This "George and Eliza Harris" figure must have been very popular, for it is
by no means rare. Why, then, this single version titled "Sailor Return"? This, I

63

85. 'Landing of the Invalided and the Wounded.' Crimean War. *Cassells Illustrated Family Paper*, 7 April 1855.

86. 'The Wounded Soldier'. *c*.1855. 10⅛ in.

87. 'Sailor Return', the only known example so titled. *c*.1855. 13¼ in.

suggest, is what may have happened. Certainly the Staffordshire modeller had seen the print and used it as a source for the "Wounded Soldier". His eye was then caught by the group of figures to the right, depicting a returning sailor with his wife and child. By now (1855) the fictional melodrama of *Uncle Tom's Cabin* had been superseded by the real-life melodrama of the Crimean War. The similarity of this group in the print to the "George and Eliza Harris" group is obvious. Simply changing the title to "Sailor Return" would be a quick and cheap way of producing yet another patriotic figure. The fact that only one such piece is known suggests that the idea was not considered a success and was abandoned.

It might be thought that once someone has been through every issue of these two newspapers, page by page, then the job is done and finished, but of course it isn't so. New figures turn up from time to time, so that this research is rather like painting the Forth Bridge; when you get to the end you start again.

The first group of figures ushered in by the fanfares of the new reign needed little more than the girl Queen herself to inspire them. Certainly many portraits and illustrations of her would have been in circulation at the time although the coronation was too early for the first issue of *The Illustrated London News*. I suspect that many of the figures come under Mr Key's heading of 'sometimes from taste' rather than from a drawing or print. The obvious symbols of royalty – crown, orb, sceptre, lion and unicorn, etc. – make many of the first figures of Victoria among the easiest to identify. There are exceptions.

A figure which is listed in Balston as L. E. Landon the poetess, sitting on a couch reading, turned up recently, with the addition of a crown by her side, titled "Her Majesty Queen Victoria". It is in the style of Obadiah Sherratt. The Landon attribution was incorrect and in fact the modeller has based his figure very accurately on a print that I discovered in the Victoria and Albert Museum. It is of Malibran, the famous opera singer, who died tragically young in 1836, the year before the accession. I think that the Malibran figure came first and that Sherratt slapped a crown on it and titled it Queen Victoria as a rush job to catch the market. It was probably on sale before the Duchess of Kent realized that her daughter ruled half the world and wanted a bedroom of her own. Early figures of Prince Albert in uniform are not always so easy to identify, but as he was nearly always paired with the Queen it is usually possible to match them up. The royal children are fairly easy to spot in the early years. They appear first in swaddling clothes, sometimes conveniently marked with a crown, and later cradled or dotted about on goats, ponies, dogs, knees, or laps, with equal impartiality. These early royal figures do not provide any great problems of identification. The Queen may have puzzled her ministers but not her collectors.

Another prolific source used by the potters was the lithographed cover of sheet music (89 and 90). Lithography, or the art of drawing on stone for reproduction,

88. Figures titled both "Omer Pacha" and "Sultan" were based on this engraving, which is a new source. *Cassells Illustrated Family Paper*, 1854. *c*.1854. 13 in.

was first introduced to England in 1800 and it is significant that its popularity runs roughly parallel with our figures, and for much the same reasons. Both the Staffordshire potters and the lithographic artists owed a great deal to the enormous growth of interest in entertainment of all kinds during the nineteenth century. The music-cover artists, and of course the newspaper illustrators, very often worked directly from life. The potters worked from life but indirectly through them, simplifying and adapting where they felt it necessary; their inspiration was the print wherever they found it. Before photography became well established many engravings of oil paintings were made and published and, when suitable, were also used by the potters. (91 and 92)

The music-cover illustration not only provided them with attractive clear prints, but was a ready-made guide to the popularity of the subject with the public. There is some difficulty in music-cover research because they are mostly collected in the British Museum under composers in the music section, not under artist or subject,

89. Lithograph music cover, 'The Original Polka'. By courtesy of the Victoria and Albert Museum.

90. La Polka, the dance which hit the Victorians like a bombshell. Possibly Grisi and Perrot. *c*.1844. 8 in.

although there are some covers without music in the Department of Prints and Drawings, and the theatre section of the Department of Prints and Drawings in the Victoria and Albert Museum has quite a lot. In fact theatre research is not easy and can involve a great deal of time-wasting travel. There are five important public collections available in London and one superb private one, so that it will be some time before all the possible sources have been examined.

Prints, then, are what the potter liked to use, newspaper prints, music covers, engravings of oil paintings, illustrations in books and, in spite of the difficulties of research, I believe a great many more figures will be identified in this way. However, many figures which are obviously of theatrical origin have remained stubbornly obscure, and I do not believe a print will ever be found to match some of them, because I think the prints have disappeared, part of the vast amount of ephemera which suffers this fate in all ages. Circus and fairground posters, and the little cheap halfpenny chap-books sold by hawkers, are the ones most likely to have been destroyed. There were probably others, illustrated pamphlets and ballad sheets, handbills announcing coming attractions in the visiting fair or travelling menagerie (known to this day in the theatre as 'throw-aways'). It is quite certain that some figures were made of fairground personalities, entertainers who never appeared in any of the established theatres.

91. David Garrick as Richard III in the nightmare scene. Detail from an oil painting by Hogarth, 1745. By courtesy of The Walker Art Gallery, Liverpool.

92. David Garrick as Richard III. Titled figures are extremely rare, untitled common. c.1850. $9\frac{1}{2}$ in.

Have a look at that splendid child Ellen Bright (102). She was firmly established in the affections of the public as 'The Lion Queen' and a star at sixteen (although there is a suspicion of nepotism in that she was the niece of the menagerie-owner Mr Wombwell). Her predecessor, another niece of Wombwell called Nellie Chapman, had very wisely retired to marry 'Lord' George Sanger in 1849. Ellen had a brief but spectacular career, dutifully appearing several times daily in a cage with a tiger and a lion. The performance went awry at Chatham in January 1850 when she was unwise enough to let her attention wander, turned her back, and was mauled to death by the tiger. It's no excuse of course, but, like many leading ladies before and since, her attitude towards her co-stars seems to have been rather cavalier, sitting on them, rapping them on the nose with a riding crop, forcing them to play when they weren't in the mood, and finally upstaging them. I'm pleased to report that the lion, who was called Wallace, had nothing whatever to do with it. The incident upset Queen Victoria as well as Ellen Bright and ladies were henceforth forbidden by law to become lion-tamers. In fact it had taken a great deal of persuasion to get the Queen to watch the act at all when Nellie Chapman performed it with Wombwell's at Windsor in November 1847 for the Michaelmas Fair. Her Majesty confined her visit to a gentle stroll past the cages when she and the animals regarded each other with mutual respect.

Miss Chapman was most anxious to perform before the Queen ('as seen by Her Majesty Queen Victoria at Windsor'). But Her Majesty had serious misgivings. She

Three figures by John Lloyd of Shelton. The centre figure could be 'Gentleman John Jackson', the champion prize fighter. It is unmarked but shares many characteristics with the other figures, both impressed 'Lloyd-Shelton'. *c.*1845. 10½ in. 10½ in. 11 in.　　Colour Plate 3.

93. Marshal Arnaud. *Cassell's Illustrated Family Paper*, 29 April 1854. (New source.)

94. Lord Raglan. *Cassell's Illustrated Family Paper*, 29 April 1854. (New source.)

95. Marshal Arnaud and Lord Raglan, army commanders Crimean War. *c*.1854. 7$\frac{1}{2}$ in.

96. *Illustrated London News*, 13 May 1857. (New source.)

97. Princess Royal and Prince Frederick William of Prussia. 1857. 16 in.

98. The Orphans. Marble group by Felix M. Miller. Even today a new source may still be found in the *Illustrated London News*. 20 February 1847.

MARBLE GROUP.—ORPHANS.—BY FELIX M. MILLER.

99. (*bottom right*) The Orphans. Thomas Parr. *c.*1852. 8 in.

100. 'A child rescued by its mother from an eagle's nest' by George Dawe, R.A. Exhibited at the Royal Academy 1813. By courtesy of Mr H. R. H. Woolford.

101. Based on the Dawe painting but almost certainly inspired by the melodrama *The Eagle and Child; or, A Mother's Courage*, Britannia Theatre, Hoxton, 10 October 1859. *c.*1860. 16 in.

was a devoted fan of the American lion-tamer Mr Van Amburgh (indeed she had a painting of him by Landseer, in his cage surrounded by his wild beasts). But a girl? Could that be quite safe? Or even proper? She decided to miss the performance and departed. Miss Chapman had to make do with the remainder of the royal party, which included the entire staff and pupils of Eton. Their enthusiastic reports were to prove too much for the curious Victoria and that same evening she attended a special performance ('as seen by Special Command of Her Most Gracious Majesty The Queen'). Miss Chapman of course was delighted, but seems to have overplayed considerably, treating the tiger with scant courtesy and ending her performance by 'inserting her head into the jaws of the noble lion Wallace'. It was a most disturbing display, and when Miss Chapman was presented after the performance the Queen thought she looked terrified, and questioned the girl with great concern. She was indeed terrified – but of Queen Victoria, not of the lions. At last she was allowed to take her leave, with a gold watch and strict instructions to be careful.

Prince Albert assured the Queen that it was all quite safe, as did the royal children, the mayor of Windsor, and Mr Wombwell himself. She didn't believe them, and no doubt she reminded them of it later when Nellie Chapman's successor was torn to pieces.

"The Death of the Lion Queen" makes a splendid figure, and is based on a wood-

102. Death of Ellen Bright, the Lion Queen, at Chatham. 1850. 14¾ in.

103. Unrecorded Victoria and Albert, probably made at the time of the royal visit to Ireland, 1849. 9¼ in.

cut in *The Illustrated London News* for 19 January 1850. At some stage along the line the tiger became a leopard in some versions of this figure, but the potter has succeeded in establishing Wallace's innocence beyond doubt. It comes in various stages, both coloured and white, and, in my experience, is fairly rare. However, there are many figures which must have been inspired by the fairground which are well worth looking for (104–8). Fairs and menageries visited the Potteries and it is possible that some modeller made his own sketches of the performers and worked from those, but I think it unlikely when so many posters and handbills were available to them. *The Theatrical Journal* for Wednesday, 14 October 1857 describes such posters on the walls of the town as being of 'a most gorgeous appearance' and *The Times* on 16 May in the same year describes a circus star, 'whose exploits have for some time past been pre-figured on the walls of London'. The history of popular entertainment in the nineteenth century requires a book of its own but its influence on the potters was far greater then has generally been recognized. I use the word 'entertainment' deliberately, for the theatrical taste of the times cannot always be neatly divided into categories. Astley's famous amphitheatre near Waterloo Bridge on the Surrey side of the Thames was basically more circus than theatre, but it didn't stop them producing Shakespeare on horseback. Both Drury Lane and

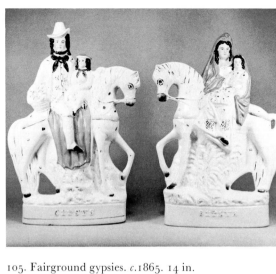

105. Fairground gypsies. *c*.1865. 14 in.

104. I used to think this was fairground or Astley's but it could well be a royal gillie in the Scottish Highlands. *c*.1850. 11 in.

106. Fortune-tellers. *c*.1850–60. 10 in. 12 in.

107. Typical Astley piece. *c*.1848. 9 in.

108. This could be a portrait taken from a print or music cover or simply a fairground theatre piece. *c.*1850. 15 in.

Covent Garden retaliated by presenting dramas with horses to bolster up box office receipts. The famous Kemble family (John Philip, Mrs Siddons and their brother Charles) made very little profit when they appeared at Covent Garden in *Hamlet, Romeo and Juliet, Macbeth* and *Othello*. A happier picture emerged when they chose to be supported by a rip-roaring 'hippodrama' called *Blue Beard; or Female Curiosity*. In this production sixteen mounted warriors charged over practical hills and bridges with 'inconceivable velocity', castles were set on fire, and dismounted warriors battled to the death over the bodies of the 'accomplished quadrupeds'. In fact the horses got rather better notices than the Kembles, who swallowed hard and made a profit of £21,000. The success of *Blue Beard* marked the end of any attempt to separate the circus from legitimate drama and the horses were to be seen at Drury Lane and Covent Garden throughout the rest of our period into the second half of the century. It seems certain that many of the rather flamboyant equestrian figures with exaggerated theatrical costumes and multicoloured saddle cloths derived from these hippodramas at Astley's, at theatres on the South Bank and at the larger legitimate theatres.

There is another large group of contemporary prints that I have sorted through hopefully for many years. At first sight they appear to hold great promise, for some

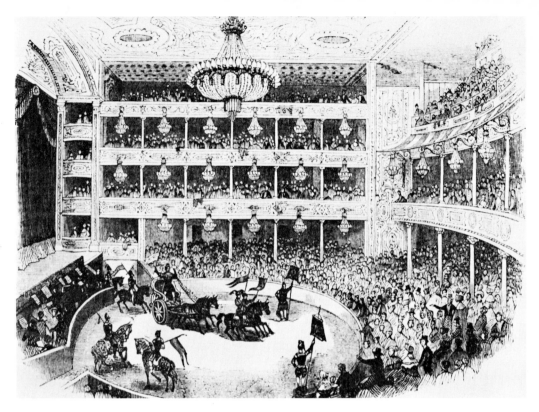

109. Astley's as it appeared from 1842 onwards. By courtesy of the Victoria and Albert Museum.

110. Blue Beard in one form or another was a great success throughout the reign. This identification was easy for his beard is bright blue. *c*.1858. $12\frac{3}{4}$ in.

111. Unidentified horsemen almost certainly Astley heroes. c.1848. $9\frac{1}{4}$ in. $8\frac{3}{4}$ in.

112. Toy Theatre print. By courtesy of the Victoria and Albert Museum.

113. Edmund Kean as Richard III. By courtesy of the Victoria and Albert Museum.

114. Edmund Kean as Richard III. c.1850. 10 in.

of them look very like our figures, but on the whole they have proved to be disappointing. The 'Penny Plain, Twopence Coloured' prints, both play sheets and and portraits, of the Toy Theatre or Juvenile Drama, first appeared about 1811. The portraits were named, and accurate both in costume and features, having been drawn from life in the theatre during performance. Some of these original drawings, with detailed notes of colour and material, may be seen in the British Museum. It has been suggested that so much care and accuracy argues that they were originally toys for grown-ups, not children; in either case, they are a valuable theatrical record.

Some of these early prints were drawn on copper plates by artists of considerable merit (both the Cruikshank brothers, Flaxman, and Dighton). The trouble is that they are too early to influence the majority of our potters. It is true that these toy-theatre sheets were reproduced from the original plates many times (either legally or pirated) and reached the height of their popularity with children between 1830 and 1840, but of course the costumes and actors were still mostly the Regency stars of a generation earlier. There were exceptions like 'The Battle of the Alma' and other Crimean war pieces in 1854, and 'Uncle Tom's Cabin' in 1852, but on the whole the toy theatre tended to live in the past. It lingered on well into the second half of the century, a delightful anachronism, but it made little appeal to the potters, to whom topicality was money. They were much more attracted to

78

115. Macready as Rob Roy Macgregor and the theatre portrait which the potter used. *c.*1848. 9¼ in.

the lithographed music covers and it was in fact the introduction of colour with chromolithography that helped to kill the hand-coloured toy-theatre prints. However, some stars and plays remained favourites well into our period, and I have been able to use these prints once or twice to identify figures, but not as many as I had hoped. A number of the single theatrical portraits were undoubtedly the potters' source for some figures, (113, 114, 115 and colour plate 5) but from the 'penny plain' sheets of characters in performance, only one untitled figure have I been able to identify with absolute certainty (116).

Melodrama, disguised as culture in the plays of the German Kotzebue, began to appear in England in the late eighteenth century. It was nourished by native English authors like 'Monk' Lewis and Mrs Radcliffe, writing glorious gothick nonsense, and finally appeared in its complete form in the translated plays of the Frenchman Pixérécourt. *A Tale of Mystery* was produced by Kemble at Covent Garden on 13 November 1802. It contained every stock ingredient of true melodrama, which influenced all forms of entertainment in England for nearly a century. (Incidentally it survived in the twentieth century in the cinema and is with us

79

116. T. P. Cooke as Long Tom Coffin in *The Pilot*, Act 1 Scene 3. The only certain identification I have ever found in a toy theatre sheet. *c.*1844. 8¼ in.

117. Minna Kitzing and Anna Selling in "*The Adventures of Flick and Flock*". Based on a Lithograph (*No. 6 Album de Bühen Costüme*) *c.*1859. 7½ in.

118. Unidentified theatre, melodrama. *c.*1850. 10½ in.

119. Unidentified theatre or opera. *c*.1850. 9¾ in.

120. Pseudo-Eastern theatrical costume. *c*.1850. 12¾ in.

122. "The Rescue", unidentified theatre melodrama. *c*.1855. 11½ in.

121. Probably T. P. Cooke as Rhoderick Dhu in *The Lady of the Lake*. *c*.1850. 11¼ in.

123. Dog hero. *c*.1860. 8 in.

124. Mr Wells, 'the popular equestrian', as John Gilpin. *c*.1845. 7 in.

125. Mr Wells as John Gilpin at Astley's. *Illustrated London News*, 28 December 1844.

today in television.) Innocence and virtue, aided by broad comic relief, were triumphant over black-hearted villainy, and virtue was rewarded. The message was delivered in every theatre in the land from Drury Lane down to the board-and-canvas theatres of the fairground.

The attempts at dress reform in the theatre made by Garrick and de Louther-bourg in the eighteenth century were slow to take effect. The feathered head-dress and passion for pseudo-Eastern costumes were to delight actors and audiences alike for many years to come (118–21). Melodrama had a thousand variations on its basic theme with heroes ranging from honest British tars (122) to dogs (123) and horses (124 and 125). It was thundered out by hooves and cannons at Astley's. It passed from the theatre into real life and back again.

The Crimean War was itself a melodrama, with the virtuous Queen, black-hearted Czar, and heroic soldiers and sailors (126, 127). The real battle of the Alma was fought in the Crimea on 20 September 1854 and again at Astley's in the following October. The stage 'Battle of Waterloo' had been a favourite since 1824 (when it was seen by the Duke of Wellington) until well into the second half of the century. The actor Gomersal astounded everyone by his likeness to the Emperor, and spent the greater part of his acting career playing nothing else; critics proclaimed it, 'a nightly theme of admiration' and 'a masterpiece of imitation'. Thackeray's Colonel Newcome 'was amazed – amazed, by Jove, Sir – at the prodigious likeness of the principal actor to the Emperor Napoleon'. There were more Staffordshire figures made of Napoleon I than of any other single personality. It is possible that some of them were intended for exportation to the French market but I have not been able to find any conclusive evidence to support this theory. Hundreds of thousands of them have survived in England but I have only ever seen five or six of them in France and these could well have found their way there later.

A working potter (C. Shaw) has recorded that in 1840 Napoleon was

> a leading article of our industry at this toy factory. . . . He stood up with arms folded across his breast, his right leg a little forward, looking defiance at his own English makers. . . . These Napoleons must have been in large demand somewhere, for shoals of them were made at this time (131).

The 'large demand' must surely have been created by the many theatrical presentations of Napoleon's campaigns both at Astley's and other theatres. A dramatic moment in one such production at Covent Garden was recorded in *The Times* on 17 May 1831. 'Buonaparte appears upon his celebrated white charger, and rides half way up the rock, the curtain falling just as he assumes that posture which the picture, representing this event, has made universally familiar.' It is interesting to compare this account with the figure of the Emperor on horseback

126. Crimean War soldier and sailor. A popular group was sometimes adapted to produce single figures. *c.*1855. 13½ in.

127. Victory over the Russian bear. *c.*1856. 11½ in.

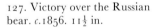

128. A unique memorial to a British soldier, Sam Barke, who died in Florence Nightingale's hospital at Scutari in the Crimea. Staffordshire porcelain made by Lockett Baguley and Cooper of Shelton. 1855. 17 in.

(132). The date is too early for this figure, but it is reasonable to suppose that such a '*coup de théâtre*' might well have been repeated later. (*The Times* thought it the best part of the play.) The print of the original French painting by David was very popular. It later appeared on a music cover and all these sources would have encouraged and inspired the potters.

The potters knew all about Good and Evil. Melodrama was life and war glamorized, not life as they had to suffer it in reality. Wesley had preached that

"The Victory". *c.*1856. 14¼ in.   Colour Plate 4

Mr GOMERSAL as NAPOLEON BUONAPARTE, Nº14.
IN THE BATTLE OF WATERLOO.
Printed & Sold by A. PARK, 47, Leonard St. Tabernacle Walk. HORSES.

129. 'Mr Gomersal as Napoleon Buonaparte.' By courtesy of the Victoria and Albert Museum.

130. One of the rarest and most splendid of all Victorian Staffordshire figures; only three are known to exist. *c.*1845. 24 in.

131. Napoleon I. Probably made by George Hood, Highgate Pottery, Tunstall. *c.*1845. 7 in.

132. "Napoleon crossing the Alps". The potters' version of the famous painting by David. *c.*1845. 9¼ in.

virtue would be rewarded in another world: melodrama went one better and promised it in this. All this was their England, recorded in the cheap and popular illustrations of the day, only some of which have survived. C. Shaw remembers the walls of his village dame school displaying pictures 'of the usual garish sort, blazing with colour and all the figures upon them in strikingly dramatic attitudes'. Our Staffordshire figures are more durable than the prints which inspired them and if we cannot identify all of them positively, their origin and spirit are as clear as their bright enamel colours.

ﻬ 6 ﻬ

Identification (Part 2)

To find the original print which a potter has obviously used for his inspiration can be both exciting and satisfying, making, as it does, the identification of an untitled figure almost certain.

However, as we have seen, some original sources may well have disappeared for ever. This does not necessarily mean that a figure is condemned to perpetual anonymity; it is possible to approach the problem from another angle.

The method combines the best features of a first-class detective story and a good crossword puzzle. The clues are all enigmatically displayed in the figure itself, waiting to help, hinder, confuse, or to set the researcher on the right path.

Of course the potters didn't think of such things as clues to be solved by future generations of collectors. For them, and for their first customers, there was no puzzle or mystery at all. Everyone knew exactly what the untitled figure was intended to represent.

What are the clues? Costume; style of potting; palette; but, most important of all, *the action of the figure, and any objects shown in connection with that action.* It is worth remembering that such objects were seldom, if ever, included purely for decorative reasons. There are of course many decorative features in Staffordshire figures but with practice it soon becomes possible to recognize these and not be misled by them. Flowers in pots, posies in hands, dogs, sheep, and rabbits, do not as a rule interest me half as much as swords, scrolls, or indeed any curious object included for no apparent reason.

It is astonishing that so many of these figures which would have been instantly recognizable not much over a hundred years ago, should have become mysterious so quickly. It would seem that we know more about the folk art of the ancient Egyptians than we do of our own in the last century. I am not grumbling that it should be so. Solving some of the puzzles has given me great pleasure for many years past, and the supply is not likely to run out for many years to come.

One of the biggest influences on the potter was the world of entertainment (see Chapters 1 and 9) and it is this, and most particularly theatre or opera, which I always consider first when confronted with a mystery figure. The reason is simple. Illustrations disappear, but a successful play, likely to have attracted the attention of the potters, nearly always survives in print. Pictures can be painted just as accurately in words as with a brush, and in this lies the importance of the original play as a source.

133. Gardeners. *c*.1860. 11 in.

134. Unidentified but a nice set of clues. *c*.1855. 12¼ in.

135. Unidentified, probably opera or ballet. The beribboned hat and the handkerchief are the clues. *c*.1845. 6¾ in.

136. Unidentified. Probably theatre or fairground. *c*.1840. 5 in. (I have recently seen a matching pair with a girl).

90

137. Empress Eugénie with the Prince Imperial. *c.*1856. 8 in.

138. Newly discovered source for 137. *Cassell's Illustrated Family Paper*, 26 July 1856.

139. Identified in *The Connoisseur*,
Jan.–April 1911, as Fanny Elssler
doing her famous castanet dance, but
it is more likely to be her sister
Thérèse who often danced the male
role. The pair would be Fanny.
*c.*1845. 8 in.

140. Giaffier. 'Thus like a Christian
flag I rend his edict'. *c.*1847. 8 in.

Even when a published copy of the play has not survived it is usually possible to
trace a manuscript copy in the office of the Lord Chamberlain or the Larpent
Collection, which is now in the Huntington Library in America. The licensing
act of 1737 required that copies of all plays should be submitted to the Lord
Chamberlain for his approval before production and that these copies should be
retained by him and preserved. This law remained basically unaltered right up to
1968. The written archives of our theatre period, therefore, are far more complete
than those which survive as illustrations. As an additional link in the chain of

evidence they can be an invaluable aid to identification.

This was the method I used to identify the figure of Madame Vestris (8). With her predilection for 'breeches parts', Vestris was one of the first tentative identifications which occurred to me when confronted by an obviously female figure potted about 1820 and dressed up as a man. A short list of plays in which she appeared at that time pointed to *Paul and Virginia*. Prints of her in costume as Paul strengthened the possibility, but it was not until I went back to the original text of the particular version in which she played that I felt I could identify the figure with any certainty without an exactly matching print (Chapter 1 page 6). Let us follow the method in closer detail and see how it works in practice.

The Turkish figure with the deed or scroll (140) had intrigued and puzzled me for many years. It had also puzzled everyone I questioned about it, for nobody knew who it was. Apart from the Crimean War, and a few other obvious exceptions, any oriental or exotic costume suggests the possibility of a theatrical origin. The annoying thing about this figure was that in the back of my mind I believed I had seen a print of something similar if not identical – possibly a toy-theatre portrait. Through the years I have known this feeling many times, and I regret to say I have nearly always been wrong. I can only assume that so great has been my desire to identify a figure that my imagination has obligingly invented prints to order. On the whole therefore, it is a feeling I have learned to treat with great caution.

The style of potting strongly suggested the first decade of Victoria's reign. Modelled in the round, it has no separate supporting pillar as in the pre-Victorian figures, but a full cloak falling from the shoulders to the ground which serves the same purpose. This cloak technique often occurs in the 1840s. Later it was to shrink to the waist at the back and finally disappear into the familiar flat back (although as usual there is considerable overlapping of styles) (54–57). The jewelled turban and ermine edge to the cloak suggested a man of importance, possibly even royal – and then there was that scroll.

The body is porcellaneous with lavish underglaze cobalt blue, generous gilding and six different overglaze enamel colours. In all it is a good example of the period. A careful search through all the theatre prints of the decade I could find failed to reveal anything similar to the scroll. There were hundreds of actors in eastern costume but the scroll, I felt certain, was the vital clue. The story began like this. One day early in 1967 I happened to see a Staffordshire pottery plate, the centre of which was decorated with a transfer print (141). The eastern costume could have been purely decorative, but on the back of the plate in a cartouche I read ' "Byron Gallery" Bride of Abydos' (142). Had I known that this was to be the beginning of the right road and not yet another dead end, I might have muttered happily 'Come Watson, the game's afoot.' But at that moment I did not know that this was to be the first real clue.

141. *c.*1840. Diameter 10½ in.

142. The back of the plate (141).

94

Lord Byron's original poem *The Bride of Abydos* was first published in 1813. It is a splendid piece of pseudo-oriental nonsense, complete with gentle, idiotic heroine, wronged hero, villainous father, pirates, bloody combats, tragic ending, and more than a hint of fashionable incest thrown in for good measure.

> 'But first – Oh! never wed another –
> Zuleika! I am not thy brother!'

In fact some of Byron's verse in *The Bride of Abydos* is more reminiscent of his namesake H. J. Byron, the pantomime king, than that of a major poet. This, for example, is how he describes his hero's tragic death.

> Fast from his breast the blood is bubbling
> The whiteness of the sea foam troubling –
> If aught his lips essayed to groan,
> The rushing billows choked the tone!

However, what I did find extremely interesting was the reference in the poem to a 'firman', which I learned was a decree emanating from the Turkish government. True, in the poem it receives only passing reference, but there it is – the villain, Giaffier, had been sent a firman by the Sultan (or Amurath). It was a straw in the wind but worth remembering.

'A long shot, Watson; a very long shot!'

The first illustrated edition of Byron's poem was published in 1838, much nearer our period, and was called 'The Byron Gallery'. In it, sure enough, I found the potter's source for the pottery plate illustration, reproduced exactly, and this time naming the characters. It was painted by De Caisne, engraved by Sangster, and titled 'Selim and Zuleika'. There was, sadly, no print of Giaffier, with or without his firman. However, the name 'Selim' struck a chord and I was sure that I had at some time seen a print of Edmund Kean as Selim. I might well have imagined the print, but to remember an actor's name made me think that I really must have seen it somewhere. The point was important, for it argued that Byron's poem had been dramatized and performed. True, the play must have been almost contemporary with the poem for Edmund Kean to have played the young hero, but if successful the play might have been revived in our period.

And so it proved. I found that not only had the poem been dramatized, but that it had been a great success, and revived many times both in London and in the provinces. In spite of this I found no useful prints of these later productions and it was the first production of the play at Drury Lane on 5 February 1818 that produced the toy-theatre portrait of 'Mr Kean as Selim'. But where, if anywhere, had I seen the other print which reminded me of the Staffordshire figure with the scroll, which might or might not be a firman? There was nothing for it but to work my

JAMESON'S THEATRICAL PORTRAITS

Published Feb. 18. 1818
by J.H.Jameson

N. 13 Dukes Court
Bow Str.

Mr. H. JOHNSTON as GIAFFIER
(In the Bride of Abydos)

"Dares the ungrateful Amurath to me, dispatch his vain Firman?"

143. By courtesy of The British Museum.

144. Selim and Zuleika. 'Encircle with free arm Zuleika's form'. c.1847. 7⅛ in. In the collection of Surgeon Captain P. D. G. Pugh.

145. Giaffier and Zuleika. 'For my sake, pardon him, I kneel to pray thee.' c.1847. 12¾ in. In the collection of Surgeon Captain P. D. G. Pugh.

way slowly through all the toy-theatre collections, both public and private, to which I had access. It took many miles of travelling, and many hours of pleasant work, during which I found the answer to some other puzzles, but not the one I sought.

I left the Print Room of the British Museum to the last, reasoning that this was the collection most likely to have been searched thoroughly by others before me. However, I was wrong; for it was here, over a year after the first clue, that I found my print. Mr. H. Johnston as Giaffier, drawn by G. Cruikshank, published 1818 and, for good measure, with a quotation from the play which was not in the poem.

> Dares the ungrateful Amurath to *me*
> Dispatch his vain Firman?
>
> (143).

I knew that the figure was not based on this first production but on the same scene with a different actor in a different costume at a later date. However, the scroll and the firman were surely the same.

'But here, unless I am mistaken Watson, is our client'.

97

The difference in costume between the print and the figure was not a case of the potter adapting, as he had with "The Victory", for the style of potting clearly pointed to the 1840s (see Chapter 4). However, I had already failed to find any matching prints from these later revivals. The time had come to use my own method and read the original text of the play. In addition, if one dramatic moment had caught the eye of the potter, why not more?

Dimond's play was published in 1818, the year of its first performance at Drury Lane, and by the standards of the day was a good workmanlike job. In a preface he explains that in Byron's poem '. . . the characters and incidents, though admirable all, were not sufficiently numerous and busy to supply the material of a stage representation continuing for three hours'.

Like Cobb, Dimond was worried about the tragic ending. Blood and thunder yes, but love and virtue must be seen to be rewarded. There were horrors enough in real life – the theatre was an escape where 'it would all come right in the end'.

> The catastrophe of the Poem [says Dimond] so magnificent in its meloncoly – so appalling in its horror, was altogether unfitted for a dramatick purpose. An incident from '*The Corsair*' (another of Byron's poems) was made the substitute. This, as I take it, though a *liberty*, was not an *outrage*. I but ventured to change the position of the harp; the hand of the same master continued to sweep its strings.

And very nicely put too, although in truth Dimond's contribution was greater than his preface modestly suggests. In this stage version the plot is briefly this. Zuleika and Selim are supposedly brother and sister – an interesting relationship, as when they are alone together he can hardly keep his hands off her. Their father, Giaffier, the Pacha of Abydos in Turkey, is the villain. He has killed his own brother, the true Pacha, who was in fact Selim's father, thus making Zuleika and Selim first cousins, which doesn't count. It is not easy to see why Giaffier spared his nephew Selim, because he is quite beastly to him all through the play, and Zuleika spends a good deal of time on her knees pleading with one or the other of them. There is in fact a suggestion of something more than parental affection in Giaffier's love for his daughter.

A new Sultan (or Amurath) ascends the throne of Turkey. He is not content to condone Giaffier's crime of fratricide, as was his predecessor, and sends the firman which upsets our villain so much. Giaffier's answer is to arrange a marriage between his daughter Zuleika (the Bride of Abydos) and fat old Osman Bey, whose army, combined with Giaffier's own, will be strong enough to defeat the Amurath. The rest of the plot need not concern us in detail but certainly gives value for money, with pirates, pageantry, dancing girls, disguises, the return of Selim's true father, Abdallah, from the dead, and a stunning finale.

All collectors will have shared the experience of looking at an interesting figure and thinking 'It *must* be a portrait, I'm sure its meant to be someone, but who?' Many of these figures strongly suggest a theatrical origin, and of these a great number wear Turkish costumes. I keep a file of photographs of such figures and, with this beside me, I now began to read Dimond's play. In the past the method has often helped me to identify a puzzling figure, so that I am always optimistic, but even I was not prepared for what followed. No less than four of the photographs were of figures, the action of which fitted so exactly into the plot of the play, that there can be little doubt of their origin. In spite of the absence of a matching print it was possible to identify all four figures as portraits from Dimond's *Bride of Abydos*.

The man who I knew would share my excitement to the full was Surgeon Captain P. D. G. Pugh, and when I felt the evidence was complete I sent it to him. His interest was immediate. He knew the figures well of course, but not their identity. What *he* had found was yet another figure, badly damaged, but clearly titled 'Bride of Abydos', and this figure too clicked firmly into place within the action of the play. All five figures are illustrated here together with the extracts from the text which describe them, and in the order in which they appear in the play. I could have quoted the bare line of relevant dialogue, but to take it out of context would not do the method justice. Apart from that, a fair chunk of the text evokes the atmosphere of nineteenth-century melodrama very well. I have cut a bit, but nothing important. So this is our play, and these are our figures, no longer anonymous but splendid gaudy bits of frozen action, like the still photographs outside a modern cinema. All the quotations and references are taken from the first (1818) edition of Dimond's play in the British Museum.

Act I. Scene II.
(*The Asiatic bank of the Hellespont on the European side. . . .* SELIM *leading* ZULEIKA, *suddenly emerges from a cypress grove on one side of the stage, and when he reaches the open space, pauses in enthusiastic contemplation of the scene.*)
SELIM:
  Oh! that the blissful now might stand for ever!
  Earth crowned with bloom and glittering in dew –
  High heaven's illimitable arch – all glory!
  And ocean, as God's glass, reflecting each –
  Perfection new! and beauty infinite!
  Thus, from this searching point, at dawn to gaze,
  Encircle with free arm Zuleika's form,
  And pour delighted eyes o'er boundless space –
  'Tis ecstasy! said I not rightly sister?
  Ah! that the blissful now might stand for ever! (144).

Having established that Selim's interest in Zuleika is more than brotherly, we move on to hear Giaffier tell his daughter, in front of Selim, that she must marry Osman Bey, whose army can save Giaffier from the wrath of the Amurath.

Act I. Scene III.

ZULEIKA:
> The Bride of Osman! Father, must this be?

(SELIM *rushes with impetuosity forward.*)

SELIM:
> No! by the prophet, no! Zuleika hold!
> Disclaim the fatal vow . . . pronounce it not.

GIAFFIER:
> Thou frenzied wretch! wilt rush upon my rage?

SELIM:
> I reck not of thee, nor of human sway
> Zuleika is the life in which I live;
> My sister! Angel! Hear! forsake me not!

ZULEIKA:
> Thou rash one! feel my love in this embrace.

SELIM:
> It is our last? Yea, so a father dooms
> Bride of Abydos! Osman's bride! Farewell. . . .

(*with a look and a gesture of distraction he rushes from the chamber.*)

ZULEIKA:
> Speak to me father, or my spirits freeze. . . .
> Nay let me hear the voice of comfort swift!

GIAFFIER:
> Thou trembling tenderness! appease thy fears
> A brawler's fit of frantic spleen – no more. . . .
> But with such punishments, I'll tame the madman!

ZULEIKA: (*eagerly*)
> For my sake, pardon him, I kneel to pray thee.

GIAFFIER: (*after a moments indecision, raises her*)
> Thou sway'st my will in all; e'en take thy pray'r.
> (*Flourish of trumpets without.*) (145).

The trumpets of course are to announce the arrival of fat old Osman, complete with his army, which cheers Giaffier up considerably. This is obviously an inopportune moment for the Amurath's emissary Bensalla to arrive, but arrive he does, complete with firman.

William Charles Macready as 'Rob Roy Macgregor'. *c.*1848. 9¼ in. See also 115.   Colour Plate 5.

Act II. Scene I.
(*Enter* GIAFFIER, OSMAN *followed by guards who drag* BENSALLA *bound.*)
GIAFFIER:

> Ply him with tortures till his sinews crack!
> Thou wretched minion of a boastful lord,
> Fire and rack shall be thy journey's fee.
> Dares the ungrateful Amurath to *me*
> Dispatch his vain Firman? bid me resign
> My Pachalick, and like an abject Greek
> Crouch at his footstool for the boon of life?
> Scorn and defiance blast him on his throne!
> Thus like a Christian flag I rend his edict –
> Thus in the dust I tread his vile remains,
> And thus my foot should trample on the neck
> Of him that sent it.

(140).

The two remaining figures of Zuleika kneeling to Selim both come from the following scene, which is set in Zuleika's appartment, where she is being prepared for her wedding by her female slaves.

Act II.   Scene II.
(*Female slaves advance joyously with musical instruments, others employ themselves in disposing stands of flowers. They dance with Zuleika's wedding veil and retire as* SELIM *enters.* ZULEIKA *rushes involuntarily to embrace him, but with reproachful look and folded arms he silently repels her.*)
ZULEIKA:

> How frown so sternly, and avert his eye?
> There's terror in that brow I've seen it scowl
> On Giaffier but ne'er oh ne'er on *me*
> Zuleika knew not Selim's frown till now
> He frights me – yet I will not fear him – Oh!
> Could I but dream it? Fear my Selim – never!

(*She disengages a rose from the flower stand next to her and approaches the abstracted youth with timid playfulness.*)

> This rose a message from the Bulbul bears.
> Will Selim reach for it? how! reject my flower!
> What, sullen yet? Oh churl it must not be;
> Why heaves that bosom with so wild a throb?
> Thou gentlest, dearest, hush thy stormy cares
> A sire may hate – Zuleika loves thee still!

(146)

146. Selim and Zuleika. 'This rose a message from the Bulbul bears. Will Selim search for it?
how! reject my flower!' *c*.1847. 9¾ in. In the collection of Surgeon Captain P. D. G. Pugh.

This figure is a particularly good example of the method, showing clearly as it does the rose, a musical instrument, and Selim's stern averted eye. It is at this point in the play that Selim obviously decides to get it into Zuleika's thick head once and for all that, sister or not, he is not content with sisterly love from Osman's bride. The message filters through, and four pages later she is on her knees again.

Act II.   Scene II.
ZULEIKA:
   Enough (*she kneels with sudden fervour*)
   By Mecca's shrine behold me swear
   An awful deep irrevocable vow.
   This hand shall ne'er be clasped by Selim's foe
   Nor suit, nor menace, nor danger, nor despair;
   Not all a father's rage, nor e'en commands
   From the throned Sultan thundering to destroy
   Shall bend my woman's heart or break my oath!
   Stand heaven and Selim witness to my pledge.

(147).

Strong stuff indeed, and it is interesting to note that four out of five figures are concerned with the brother/sister relationship. In the first half of the century incest held a great deal of interest in literature and drama, just as homosexuality does today. Vast families and cramped living conditions may have contributed to it, but whatever the reason the potters knew people were interested and cashed in on it.

There remains the question of which production of the play the figures came from. Tempting though it is to identify Selim as Edmund Kean, it cannot be, for Kean only played that first production at Drury Lane in 1818 and all these figures belong to the 1840s. Possibly the figure titled "Bride of Abydos" does not represent actors at all, but illustrates the original poem. The potter has based his figure on the De Caisne painting, engraved in 1838, of Byron's poem. It was no doubt the interest in the play which caused the potter to look for a source. De Caisne, of course, may have based his painting on an actual production (141). The other figures must come from Dimond's play, for they depict incidents not contained in the poem. There were notable revivals at Belfast in 1836 and Sheffield in 1840 and, not content with incest, Astley did it on horseback in London on 3 May 1847, adding, for good measure, 'camels, zebras, tiny ponies and an elephant'. There was a later revival at the Strand in 1858 but this is too late, and in any case it was done as a burlesque (with the script curiously enough by H. J. Byron). It is possible that so successful a play was pirated and performed under another name. In the toy-theatre collection of the British Museum (Vol. 5 page 21) there is a small

147. Selim and Zuleika. 'Enough! (*she kneels with sudden fervour*) By Mecca's shrine behold me swear.' *c.*1847. 11 in.

titled illustration of Giaffier tearing the firman, but the play was called *Cherry and Fair Star or The Orphans of Cyprus*. It seems likely that this was a pirated version of *The Bride of Abydos* as it was produced at Drury Lane's rival, Covent Garden, in 1822. Like the original, this play seems to have become a burlesque and ended its days later in the century as a successful pantomime. The original script is in the Larpent Collection (L 124 M). My own feeling is that the play must have been done in one form or another in provincial theatres and fairgrounds many times over and it was mainly in these audiences that the potters saw their market. It was most likely the Astley production of 3 May 1847 that first attracted their attention. With the exception, therefore, of the figure actually titled "Bride of Abydos", which is based on the Sangster engraving of the De Caisne painting (circa 1838) it seems reasonable to identify the figures as portraits of the following actors in the Astley production: Mr Barton as Giaffier; Mr Harwood as Selim; Miss Rosa Henry as Zuleika. I think it quite possible that more figures based on the play will be discovered, although the flamboyant incidents of the second half might well have defeated even the ingenuity of our potters. Collectors may now perhaps consider some of their unidentified oriental figures in a new light.

It seems hardly fair to leave poor Zuleika on her aching knees when we have followed her fortunes so closely. What would the audience who bought our figures have seen at the end of the play? The central portion we can skip but I promise you it keeps up a cracking pace with the fat old Osman battering on her door in vain, and Selim's real father, Abdallah, the true Pacha, arriving in the nick of time, disguised as a pirate chieftain. Rather than see his daughter married to Selim, the wicked Giaffier orders a slave, Murteza, to kill her. She flies to the tower of the harem which promptly catches fire in the general conflict and proceeds to explode with gratifying regularity thereafter. It is at this unsatisfactory point in the affair that our hero – now safe in the knowledge that he is only a first cousin – decides to intervene.

Act III.   Scene VII.
(*He breaks with overwhelming frenzy through all opposition and springs into the ruin. Second explosion and entire front falls down and exhibits the appartments within.* ZULEIKA *pursued is seen rushing through the fire to the head of the staircase.*)
ZULEIKA:
   Save me! my father, hear and save your child!
MURTEZA:
   You plead in vain, my oath constrains the blow.
ZULEIKA:
   Mercy!   Mercy!
(*she shrieks in frantic agony, and twists her arms round the pillar at the top of the stairs. Selim at the same moment is seen climbing towards her, she exclaims wildly.*)

ZULEIKA:

Selim!

MURTEZA:

Nor he, nor heaven saves thee now!

(MURTEZA *lifts the dagger threatening to strike. A third explosion is heard and the entire floor of the appartment gives way and sinks with* MURTEZA *into the flames below.* ZULEIKA *by clinging to the stone pillar is preserved.* SELIM *gains the head of the staircase, receiving her in his arms, and disappears with her down the steps which yet remain unbroken.*)

ABDALLAH:

Parent of mercies! guard my boy!

(SELIM *forcing his return over the perilous ruin bears* ZULEIKA *forward triumphantly.*)

SELIM:

She lives!

Delirious ecstasy! for me she lives!

Zuleika! Bride of Abydos! Selim's bride!

(GIAFFIER *who has fainted with terror at the sight of the brother he thought he had killed uncloses his eyes and rests them on his daughter whilst* ABDALLAH *joins her hand to* SELIM'S. *The pirates group triumphantly about the distance of the scene and amidst the shouts of victory the curtain falls.*)

I would very much like to have seen *The Bride of Abydos*.

❧ 7 ❧

Forming a Collection

Victorian Staffordshire is still probably the most underpriced and neglected field for collectors in the world.

There are several reasons for this. Made for a popular market, on the whole it never got much farther than the mantel-shelves of the lower middle class or the workman's cottage although there are some exceptions to this generalization. Above that level, as we have seen, came the insipidities of Wedgwood and the desperate gentility of Minton's lace knickers, and above that again the glories of Chelsea and Bow. The very fact that it was vulgar, in the true sense of the word, invoked a built-in prejudice inherent in the rigidity of the English social system. The *Punch* cartoon of 1868 reproduced here is an illuminating contemporary comment. Mr Fadsby's opinion was to remain basically unchanged for a hundred years, and Mrs Grabbit's allegiance was not to falter until the early twentieth century (148).

It was the early decades of the century which saw our figures overwhelmed by the anti-Victorian wave which swept them off the mantel-shelves into dustbins, attics and junk shops all over the country. It was the lowest ebb of the tide. A small but discerning group of collectors ignored the opinion of their contemporaries and, at that very time, began to lay the foundations of a revival which has been growing ever since. An article in *The Connoisseur* as early as 1911 (Jan-April Vol. XXIX) describes the Cecil Duncan-Jones collection of Victorian Staffordshire theatre figures. There are ten photographs and the author says,

> It is true they are becoming rare, and have to be sought in places where cobwebs are thickest. . . . In the Duncan-Jones collection there are nearly half a hundred of them, and probably there are many larger collections in England.

The average price paid then for a figure was a guinea.

It is no good looking back to those early days and thinking wistfully of the bargains to be had then. The sensible attitude for new collectors is surely to be grateful that so much remains that is good, unrecognized, and therefore still reasonably priced. After all, no one would wish to collect something that was falling in value. Figures that I believed I had paid top prices for only a few years ago now appear to have been extremely reasonable. The thing to do is look with care and imagination for the bargains to be found now, and perhaps to collect with a set plan in mind.

ÆSTHETICS.

148. Fadsby (in agony; he's a martyr to the decorative art of the Nineteenth Century). "OH! MRS.
GRABBIT—I REALLY MUST—IMPLORE YOU—TO REMOVE THOSE CHIMNEY ORNAM——UGH!—THOSE
TWO—FICTILE ABOMINATIONS—FROM THIS ROOM WHILE I REMAIN HE-AR!"
[Of all the Artis's, Mrs. Grabbit said, as she'd ever let her Apartments to, he was the most
partic'lar.
Reproduced by permission of *Punch.*

149. In the collection of Mr Timothy Manderson.

150. Naval figures, part of a private collection.

151. 'Crispins', the famous theatre restaurant in Kennington.

152. A hall. Part of a private collection of white horses.

153. General Sir George Brown. General Sir James Simpson. *c.*1854. 13 in.

154. Very rare figure of Lord Raglan. *c.*1854. $12\frac{3}{4}$ in.

155. Unidentified officers. *c.*1860. $12\frac{1}{2}$ in.

156. *c.*1854. $10\frac{1}{2}$ in. $10\frac{3}{4}$ in.

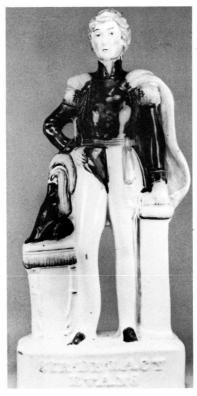

157. Admiral Sir Richard Saunders
Dundas. *c*.1855. 12½ in.

158. Sir De Lacy Evans. *c*.1854.
12½ in.

159. General Pélissier. *c*.1854. 17½ in.

161. Napoleon III. and
Albert. *c*.1854. 13¼ in.

160. Sir Colin Campbell. *c*.1854.
10½ in.

163. James Rush the murderer lived at Potash Farm, his victims and landlord at Stanfield Hall the scene of the crime. He was hanged in public outside Norwich Castle on 21 April 1849. *c*.1849. 5¼ in.

162. William Palmer poisoned his wife and his brother and his best friend. He was hanged in June 1856. *c*.1856. 11¼ in.

Of course, a collector may well decide to buy all the figures within his price range that give him pleasure to look at, and to form a general collection. I know many who have done this and their collections make a brave show in their homes. Incidentally it is most interesting to notice that, whereas a few years ago people tended to think of a Staffordshire collection as being more suitable for a country setting, more and more collectors now live in towns and large cities. Staffordshire is very good-tempered and complements many widely different settings. I have seen collections looking as completely at home in an Elizabethan music room as in a modern flat. It is quite true that, unlike many ceramics, the more Staffordshire figures you have, the better they look (152), but the time may well come when a collector will wish to specialize. It's not a bad idea to consider this at the outset.

A collection may fall into hundreds of different categories; it depends entirely on the individual taste. Nothing is more amenable or accommodating to a new collector than Staffordshire. The figures embraced the whole world of Victorian England and the possibilities are endless. One of the most fascinating centuries in history is at your feet and yours to command.

It is surely unnecessary to list all the most obvious choices, for they spring tailor-made to the mind. Soldiers, sailors, royalty, criminals, wars, actors, animals and so on. They are all capable of subdivision. Royalty can be restricted to royal

164. Charles Kean as Rolla in *Pizarro*. *c*.1860. 12¾ in.

165. A difficult figure to find. *c*.1858. 12 in.

166. Miss Rebecca Isaacs singing 'I want to be a Bloomer'. *c*.1851. 8½ in.

167. Jenny Lind as Alice in *Robert the Devil* at Her Majesty's Theatre. *c*.1847. 13½ in.

168. The American actor James Hackett as Falstaff. This one is about 1852 but many were made later. 9¾ in.

169. Maria Foote as Arinette in *The Little Jockey* made *c*.1843. 5½ in.

170. Jenny Marston and Frederick Robinson as Perdita and Florizel. *c.*1852. 11¾ in.

Unidentified, probably theatre or opera. *c.*1850. 11¼ in.   Colour Plate 6.

171. *c.*1880. 9½ in.

172. The most famous elephant in the world. Taken from the London Zoo to America by Barnum, he charged a railway train and died in September 1885. *c.*1885. 10½ in.

173. *c.*1845. 5¾ in.

174. *c.*1860. 8 in.

175. *c.*1855. 6 in.

176. *c.*1855. 5 in.

177. *c.*1855. 7¾ in.

178. *c.*1845. 7¾ in. There are many later copies.

179. Unusual. *c.*1855. 9½ in.

180. Rare. *c.*1860. 6 in.

181. Probably made as fairground toys for children, pairs are worth looking for. *c.*1865. 2½ in. to 3¾ in.

182. 'Comforter' dogs. Many copies are still being made. *c.*1860. 10½ in.

183. Empress Eugénie and Napoleon III. Coloured titled version rare. *c.*1854. 11¾ in.

184. Sir John Franklin explorer. Discovered
the North-West passage. *c.*1850. 10½ in.

185. *c.*1850. 10¾ in.

children, foreign royalty, royalty on horses, etc. Even a restricted collection has an
amiable way of spreading. A collection of naval figures will wander quite happily
into other categories: royal sailors; actors and actresses playing sailors; and ex-
plorers like Sir John Franklin and Captain Cook. Obviously a collector who is
attracted to a popular theme must expect to pay more for named or identified
figures of fine quality in good condition. They may well be no better potted or more
pleasing to the eye than figures costing much less, but they command their price
and always will. It is a fact that such figures tend to increase in value more quickly
than unnamed ones but new discoveries are being made all the time. The chance of
buying a bargain in Staffordshire is considerably greater than it is with more established antique fields. Let me give you an example.

Some time ago I bought a figure which no one knew anything about so that it
was not expensive (185). It had a sort of dotty charm and I liked it, which is the
best reason for buying Staffordshire. An identical figure had come up for sale at
Christie's in 1964. It was described in the catalogue as 'a Patriotic group, of a sailor,
drinking a pint of beer and taking leave of his legless mother' – a happy title, perhaps
owing more to imagination than research. A long search failed to find a print or a

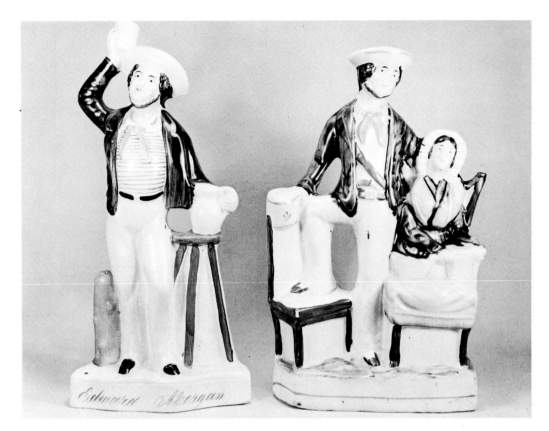

186. *c*.1850. 11½ in. 10¾ in.

music cover that looked even remotely like it. If such a print had existed – and it almost certainly had – then it had disappeared; perhaps for ever.

The next step was to examine the clues in the figure to see if they suggested the plot of a melodrama of the period. The sailor is holding what appears to be a tankard of ale (it seems safe to assume that a British sailor of the nineteenth century would be unlikely to be drinking water). The lady by his side, wearing an old woman's frilled lace cap, certainly appears to have no legs, and to be sitting on a mercifully well padded chair. Legless she may be, but her hands are well occupied, although with what is obscure.

One dealer to whom I showed it was in no doubt at all.

' "Crimean Veterans Begging",' he said firmly. 'Anyway that's what *I* sell it as. The old girl is playing a hurdy-gurdy and the son is singing. It must be her son; no sailor is going to bother with a woman of that age, especially with no legs. She must have gone out with Florrie Nightingale to do her bit and copped a cannon ball. That's it, for sure, "Crimean Veterans Begging". '

It was an intriguing theory. My partner Peter Sutton and I sat and looked at the figure with a new interest. 'So what was concealed beneath the padded chair?'

asked Sutton, who accepts very little without proof. 'Wheels,' said the dealer, and departed to catch a train, leaving us to digest his theory.

Poor old woman! The thought of those Victorian cobbled streets, and the pneumatic tyre not yet invented, was not pleasant, and a performance after the journey to boot. Certainly a legless mother playing a hurdy gurdy with a drunken son bawling ballads would have been a smash hit on any street corner. She might well need the protective arm of her son lest her furious exertions sent her hurtling into the gutter. It was some months later when Sutton found the first clue that finally demolished the Crimean Veterans.

We had just bought the rare sailor figure titled "Edward Morgan" in gilt script, and Sutton immediately said that it reminded him strongly of the sailor son. We set them side by side and certainly the similarity was striking (186). There was a definite facial resemblance and both pieces had almost certainly come from the same factory and from the hand of the same modeller. His treatment of the furniture is common to both pieces. It is true that the son has a pistol and cross-band but perhaps this would have been found in the original print.

Edward Morgan is a character in a burletta, written by Charles James Mathews (1803–78), called *He Would Be an Actor*. Unfortunately it seemed that I would not be able to use my method, for this was one instance when the original script had not survived. It was extremely frustrating, for I very much wanted to know if it had contained any reference to a legless mother.

From the *Dictionary of National Biography* I found that Mathews's reminiscences were published and edited by Charles Dickens junior. In this I found a new clue and moved a step forward. Mathews was one of the most famous and popular actors of his day and, together with his equally famous wife Madame Vestris, was a great favourite with the public. In his biography he records that Edward Morgan was originally a ballad, the words of which he had written when a young man in North Wales. In the farm-house where he had stayed was a pretty little Welsh dairymaid called Jenny Jones, and a simple plough boy named Edward Morgan.

Mathews had just heard a Welsh air played by a blind harpist, which so delighted him that he wrote 'The Ballad of Jenny Jones and Edward Morgan' to fit the music. He says,

> The Ballad I then composed to my newly discovered national air, bearing the young lady's name, has since made the interesting young couple familiar to Londoners. They would perhaps be astonished to know their history was publicly recorded and blush to find its fame.

The ballad was an instant success and, 'whistled about the streets', it remained a great favourite for many years. Mathews thought so highly of it that he later introduced it into his burletta *He Would Be an Actor* at Madame Vestris's Royal

187. Edward Morgan and Jenny Jones. Identified with the aid of a music cover of Jenny Jones in which Langolen is spelt thus. *c.*1850. 10½ in.

Olympic Theatre on the 31 October 1836. The play was a hit and ran for ninety-four performances, heading the list over all others that season. The ballad must have contributed a good deal, for after four performances the theatre bills gave it a special mention: 'Mr Charles Mathews will sing the Welsh ballad of Jenny Jones.' The burletta script was lost but the ballad survived in print. The music, I knew from the biography, was written by John Parry, and under his name I found a copy in the music library of the British Museum. It had the original lyrics, 'Written and sung by Mr Charles Mathews with the greatest success at Madame Vestris Olympic Theatre'.

> My name's Edward Morgan, I live at Llangollen
> The vale of St Tafyd the flow'r of North Wales.
> My father and mother too live at Llangollen
> Good truth I was born in that sweetest of vales.
>
> Yes indeed and all countries so foreign and beautiful
> That little valley I prize far above
> For indeed in my heart I do love that Llangollen
> And sweet Jenny Jones too in truth I do love.   (187).

The ballad goes on to describe how Edward Morgan served in the British navy and 'for twenty long years I have ploughed the salt ocean' and ends:

> I parted a lad from the vale of my Fathers
> And left Jenny Jones then a cockit young lass
> But now I'm returned a storm beaten old mariner
> Jenny from Jones into Morgan shall pass.
>
> And we'll live on our cheese and our ale in contentment
> And long thro' our dear native valley will rove
> For indeed in our hearts we both love that Llangollen
> And sweet Jenny Morgan with truth I will love.

Now for the first time the figure appears in its original identity. The frilled cap is not the lace of an old mother's bonnet but the traditional Welsh hat seen more clearly in the side view. She appears legless because she is not sitting on a chair, but at a table with her legs safe and sound underneath the table cloth. She is not playing a hurdy gurdy, but cutting a loaf of bread with a knife. With the words of the song to guide us, we can now clearly see a huge half round of cheese on the table (she was, you will remember, a dairymaid).

'And we'll live on our cheese and our ale in contentment.' In that one line lay the final clue and the puzzle was solved. Farewell to my legless mother, but welcome to a new figure of "Edward Morgan and Jenny Jones",

Now the significance of this sort of research is obvious. The figure has greatly increased in value, quite apart from the satisfaction of knowing what it is. It would be nice to claim it as a definite portrait of Charles Mathews but without a print we cannot be absolutely certain. The ballad must have been popular for many years after the burletta was forgotten, and I don't doubt was sung by many different people up and down the country. On the other hand, Mathews was a star and remained active almost until his death in 1878. A portrait figure of Mathews would certainly have sold better than a nonentity. My belief is that our figure was probably based on a music front showing a portrait of Mathews singing the ballad, *circa* 1850. In any case it is a good example of the sort of figure a new collector might well consider buying. Remember that although our potters were magnificent primitive artists, this was incidental to their main objective. They made to sell and to make money, and a figure with a story behind it sold better than a purely decorative piece. It was as simple as that. I will go further and say that many pieces of Staffordshire which for many years have been thought to be dotty-decorative, are in fact dotty-descriptive. Slowly but surely these figures are yielding to research, and every year their number grows and their value increases.

Such figures are not difficult to find and they are considerably underpriced. The

more bizarre and ludicrous the subject, the greater the likelihood of its identity being discovered. Look at the piece illustrated in 188. Now what is that intrepid lady doing up a tree being fed grapes by an Arab? What indeed? You may well ask, and I cannot tell you. You may be quite sure that she is not there purely on the whim of the potter. She is quite certainly a portrait, either of a real-life character like Lady Hester Stanhope (but I don't think so) or possibly a character in a melodrama of the day. I have seen several versions of this piece, all variations on the same theme. In one the lady is balanced side saddle on a camel with the identical Arab offering her water from an oasis well. Another has her perched elegantly, if somewhat precariously, on a bridge, again being plied with water. The other day I spotted her being offered a platter of freshly caught fish by the same Arab, whose motives remain obscure but whose persistence must command respect.

It is possible that this series of figures, and others like them in Eastern or biblical clothes, were taken from illustrated books of a high moral tone in the Sunday School libraries of the Potteries. The influence of these schools on the potters must have been considerable; in many cases they provided the only organized education the workers had ever known. As illiteracy was almost universal, it seems reasonable

189. Flight to Egypt. *c.*1855. 9½ in.

190. Abraham and Isaac. *c.*1860. 12 in.

191. *c.*1860. 11¼ in.

Saul Presenting his Daughter to David

Colourful Biblical groups,
a neglected field for collectors.

126

to assume that the religious books used would have contained many illustrations suitable for conversion into clay. Perhaps some of the non-conformist sects have kept records of those early libraries; if so they would make interesting material for research. Again, I don't know when the custom of giving children books for Sunday School prizes originated. Certainly when I was a regular, if reluctant, pupil of the Primitive Methodist Sunday School in Abersychan in the 1920s it was well established. Both my brother and I received books full of detergent-white Christs performing miracles, as had our father before us from the same source. Father's prizes came at the latter end of the nineteenth century, and I have no reason to suppose that they would have changed very much from the 1850s. Such illustrated books, when they were not purely biblical, tended towards cautionary advice. I remember the titles of two of my father's prizes as they sat side by side in the bookcase at home, *Effie's Temptation* and *Willie's Ordeal*. I can't remember what tempted Effie, or what horrors Willie had to endure, but I wish I had them still, they might well have solved a few puzzles for me.

Some of the religious groups are most attractive, very well potted with clean bright colours. At the moment they are very reasonably priced and a most neglected field for collectors (189, 190 and 191).

In spite of their non-conformist background, the potters were certainly happy to make Catholic figures if they thought they would sell. Portrait figures of successful ministers, both Catholic and Protestant, were very popular, although they are harder to find and more expensive. The Church of England, being the Established Church and thus linked with authority and government, was largely ignored. Some of the holy water stoups and crucifixion figures (31) were obviously intended for areas with large Catholic communities like Liverpool. There was, however, a small group of Catholics in the Potteries, and there are small charming figures of Sister Margaret Mary Hallahan and Père Bernard Moulaert, both of whom worked at Longton and Stone about 1850 (192). The Theatre and the Church have always had a great deal in common and a powerful appeal, the Church having a slight edge perhaps, with the advantage of a consistently good script. If the Devil promoted the stars of the Theatre, God was fighting a strong rearguard action with His own stars of the Church.

In July 1843 there arrived from Ireland such a star. Father Theobald Mathew was known as 'The Apostle of Temperance'. An Irish priest of gentle but compelling personality, he had in 1838 persuaded huge numbers of the Irish to give up all alcohol and take a pledge of total abstinence. A powerful star of God indeed! His advance notices in the English newspapers were impressive. 'He is gifted with all the qualities adapted to gain and retain ascendancy over the multitude.' 'By his exertions a great moral revolution has been wrought and a nation has been regenerated.' *The Illustrated London News* went so far as to compare him in influence

192. Sister Margaret Mary Hallahan and Père Bernard Moulaert. *c.*1850. About 3 in.

with Luther and Knox. With such a reputation, had he failed in England, he had a long way to fall.

In the event God needn't have worried, for Father Mathew did Him proud. At his first open air meeting at Commercial Road East the crowd exceeded sixty thousand. A temporary platform collapsed with fifty people on it and was hastily re-erected in time for the star to be introduced by Earl Stanhope, a resolute abstainer for many years. Torrential rain did nothing to dampen the ardour of the crowd. All through the long day they came forward in groups and knelt in the mud under the upraised arm of the Apostle of Temperance, and forswore alcohol for ever. 'Among those who took the pledge', said an observant eye witness, 'were many with black eyes and bruised faces who appeared to have been making great sacrifices to Bacchus.' The harder it rained, the more they clamoured for his blessing. Over three thousand of them made the solemn vow; they included several policemen, the recruiting sergeant of the 21st Regiment, and a Highland piper in full costume. Earl Stanhope got so carried away that he took the pledge all over again, was promptly embraced by Father Mathew and got a smacking great kiss on the cheek. In short a good time was had by all and the meeting was a huge success. It was to set the pattern for a triumphant, nation-wide tour, and its

193. Father Theobald
Mathew. *c.*1843. 5⅛ in.

significance was not lost on the potters.

It has been said that the portrait figures of this period, 1840–45, show no recognizable likeness to their subjects, but the little figure of Father Mathew giving his blessing (193) is remarkably like the drawings of him in *The Illustrated London News* for August 1843. There are several versions of this figure, all of them quite small, about five inches. I am tempted to think that the potters, ever practical, made them small to enable large numbers of them to be hawked among the crowds attending the meetings. Thousands of them must have been made, and it's just the sort of unnamed figure which could still turn up in a junk shop, although it appears to be quite rare. The arm upraised in benediction is very vulnerable and is nearly always broken, so that one in good condition is very desirable. He would fit equally well into a collection of 'Religion' or 'Personalities of the Nineteenth Century'.

I think the great thing about starting a new collection is to bring a completely open mind to your choice. You are more likely to collect well for a modest outlay in a field of your own choosing, than by buying where the competition of other collectors is keenest. Given that the basic condition is good, and that it is not a fake or a reproduction, there is no earthly reason why you shouldn't have the best collection of, say, tartan skirts in the world.

The illustration (194) is a good example of what may be achieved by a new

129

194. In the collection of Mrs Bunty Jones.

195. *c*.1855. 13 in.

collector with imagination and enthusiasm. This lady decided to limit her collection of Staffordshire figures to those that portrayed musical instruments or singers. She began collecting in January 1970, and in five months she had bought all the figures shown here. She was sensible enough to seek advice from a knowledgeable collector, and so was able to avoid wasting money on modern reproductions or forgeries. For a comparatively modest outlay she has formed a most attractive colourful collection, united by a simple original idea.

I have always rather liked what I call 'boat figures' and I mention them here as another example of the sort of category one can invent for a collection. Quite a lot of them were made and many will probably be found to be theatre or fairground melodrama (196–199). Certainly the single sailor figures in boats may well have their origin in the stage convention which demanded that the sailor hero should sail to the rescue and land from a little boat – doubtless pulled by ropes (195). Victorian Staffordshire animals inspired by the travelling menageries are a fraction of the price of eighteenth-century animal figures and look splendid gathered together (200, 201 and 202).

Figures that incorporate imitation clock faces and watch holders could form a delightful collection (203, 204, 205 and 227). These were made for poor working people who could not afford the luxury of a real mantel-shelf clock. It has been

196. c.1845. 7½ in. c.1850. 7½ in.

197. c.1825. 7½ in.

198. c.1845. 7 in.

199. c.1860. 12½ in.

Boat figures.

132

Marietta Alboni in Rossini's *La Cenerentola. c.*1848. 9 in.   Colour Plate 7.

200. *c.*1860. $7\frac{1}{2}$ in.

201. *c.*1860. $7\frac{1}{2}$ in.

202. Isaac Van Amburgh, the American lion-tamer, made a lion lie down with a lamb. *c.*1848. $10\frac{1}{4}$ in.

203. St George and the Dragon (theatrical). *c.*1845. 11 in.

204. Rare Romeo and Juliet. *c.*1845. 12 in.

205. Napoleon I and Wellington. *c.*1845. 9 in.

206. "Babes in the Wood". double spill vase. c.1845. 7¼ in.

said that these 'clocks' usually showed 'tea time' in case a neighbour should drop in for a cup of tea. It is a pleasant story, but reluctantly I must record that I have seen the hands painted at almost every hour of the day. Later, when even poor people could afford a pocket watch, some splendid figures appeared that served as watch holders, and the mantel-shelf clock became a reality in their homes. Very occasionally separate pottery watches may be found. These were used to slip into the watch holder when the real watch was being used by the man of the house.

Matches were expensive, but the fire in the kitchen range was alight all day, summer and winter. Children rolled spills out of scraps of old paper to light candles, paraffin lamps, and father's pipe. The spills were kept on the mantel-shelf in figures specially designed to hold them. They could form a colourful collection of great variety (201, 206).

The great thing is not to be hide-bound by convention. Probably no other field of antiques gives the collector such variety of choice. Figures with dogs. Figures with weapons (rifles, pistols, bows and arrows, clubs, swords, daggers, bagpipes). Figures with flags would make a splendid array (209–213) – the possibilities are limited only by the imagination of the individual collector. Any category once decided upon may bring into the net a rare figure, perhaps even one which will be identified later on as a definite portrait, and an important discovery.

135

207. Probably the royal children. *c*.1850. 7¾ in.

208. Probably the royal children. *c*.1850. 10 in.

136

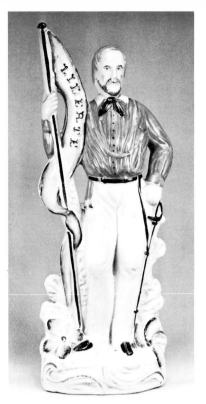

211. The Anglo-French war scare. *c.*1860. 12 in.

209. Crimean War. *c.*1854. 11½ in.

210. Garibaldi. *c.*1864. 13¼ in.

212. "Sailor's Dream". *c.*1854. 8 in.

213. "Soldier's Dream". *c.*1854. 13¾ in.

Flag figures

214. 'And we'll live on our cheese and our ale in contentment . . .' Undated music cover.

Some time ago, when I was writing about the "Edward Morgan and Jenny Jones" figure, Surgeon Captain Pugh came into the shop and I told him about the work I had done on it and my conclusions. He agreed with the identification, and we both wondered if indeed the original print was lost for ever, or would one day be found. A few days later he telephoned me and said that since our conversation he had been offered some music covers, which he had bought. Among them, by a quite extraordinary coincidence, was the missing source which my research had convinced me had existed, but which I thought had disappeared. I am grateful for his permission to reproduce it here (214). It still doesn't prove the figure to be a portrait of Mathews, for the print doesn't mention his name. It does however prove, in a most gratifying way, that my method of identifying untitled figures can be accurate. I was particularly pleased to see that the very line from the ballad which gave me my final clue is reproduced in the printed verse below the music cover:

'And we'll live on our cheese and our ale in contentment'

This music cover had been known for some years to be the source for the titled figure of "Edward Morgan" but I had never seen it. I had not realized, therefore, that it was also the source I was seeking for the 'Legless Mother' figure. Nothing is perfect, however, and the pistol and cross-band remain a minor mystery; an added touch of the potter's imagination perhaps. Such research can be most enjoyable for collectors and I cannot think of a more satisfying way to end this chapter.

💫 8 💫

Fakes, Forgeries, Reproductions and Restorations

Throughout the ages any art form which has become popular and sought after by collectors has, sooner or later, received the attention of the forger and the faker. This has now happened with Victorian Staffordshire figures. It is of course a compliment, the final accolade; but it scares the hell out of new collectors and it need not.

Over and over again people ask me, 'How do you know a figure is genuine?' How indeed? The short answer is, 'Experience', but that's not much help if you haven't got any. One of the aims of this book is to help collectors who have no experience, people who don't want to throw money away on a reproduction, or worse still a forgery or a fake. So let us take it as slowly and plainly as we can. First, let us define terms.

Reproductions.

A reproduction is the easiest to understand. It is a figure made at a later date, sometimes, but not always, from the original mould. Reproductions are usually made in Staffordshire by reputable honest potters without intent to deceive. They have been made more or less continuously throughout this century and are still being made today. What happens when an honest reproduction falls into the hands of an ignorant or dishonest dealer is a different matter. They then in effect become fakes. Even if they have not been physically changed, they are nevertheless fakes, because they are offered for sale as genuine, and are therefore changed in the eye of the inexperienced collector who has misplaced his trust.

Strictly speaking, the first reproductions were made in the last quarter of the nineteenth century. Take the Tallis-type figures for instance. From the evidence of the subjects potted, the dates of the original figures would seem to cover a period of roughly twenty years, from 1850 to 1870. There is some confusion of evidence, but shortly after 1870 the Tallis-type master moulds appear to have been used by a Burslem potter called John Parr, who worked from 1870 to 1879. After a partnership between Parr and another Burslem potter, William Kent, which lasted from 1880 to 1894, they passed into the control of Kent, whose sons and grandson continued to reproduce figures from them (with short breaks during wartime) until 1962. Some of the Kent moulds then passed to the Blakeney Art Pottery in

215. "Turkey England France" and Napoleon III. c.1854. 10¼ in.

216. Prince Alfred. c.1858. 7¼ in. 5 in. 3½ in.

217. Very rare Nelson and Victory. c.1843. 5½ in.

142

The figures in (215), (216) and (217) are all genuine.

218. Made by Thomas Parr. *c.*1852. 10½ in.

219. Probably made by John Parr. *c.*1870. 10½ in.

Stoke-on-Trent where they have been converted to slip or cast moulds and figures are still being reproduced from them today (1971)

Surgeon Captain Pugh has suggested to me that John Parr could well have obtained the original moulds from another potter called Thomas Parr who was working in Burslem from 1852 to 1870, almost the exact period covered by the original figures. It would seem, therefore, that Tallis-type figures could be more accurately described as Parr-Kent figures. The earliest of these figures made by Thomas Parr were potted with the characteristics I have described in Chapter 5. The finished figure was the nearest the Staffordshire potter ever came to rivalling the modelling, if not the body, of porcelain. But perhaps the most certain guide to these original figures is the quality of the decoration, in particular the small floral pattern painting to be found on some of them. A good example is the dress skirt of Juliet in the figure showing the lovers played by the American Cushman sisters (218). Hundreds of minute brush strokes have been used to build up the pattern which, for delicacy and painstaking care, can stand comparison with the best efforts of the major porcelain factories of the day. Hair was rendered with a distinctive combed effect not found in the products of less sophisticated potters. The glaze was superb, bright and clear, giving such a fine luminous quality to the enamel colours that it

220. "The Soldier's Farewell". Made by Kent and Parr. *c.*1880. 8½ in.

is difficult to believe that they do not lie beneath its surface completely.

There is no positive proof that all these original figures were accorded the same high quality of decoration and finish, but at least we can say that those which have it are of unquestionable authenticity. The Cushman sisters and many other Parr-Kent figures are sometimes found in excellent quality but just lacking this highest standard. Very often Juliet's dress is much plainer, the bodice decorated with touches of gold, and the skirt relieved only by a pale pink in the folds (219). In all other respects these figures are almost, but not quite, as good as the others. Now it is possible that this second-class quality was contemporary with the first-class figures, but unfortunately no original price list exists to help us. We simply do not know. Both states are good, but one is certainly superior. My own feeling is that the second-quality figures could well be the work of John Parr or Parr and Kent, while the original fine figures are the work of Thomas Parr.

There is a third category of Parr-Kent figure. Again excellently potted with most of the characteristics including the fine streaked brush strokes of the base. But there is a major difference: the palette has changed; the enamel colours are not the same. They are stronger, deeper and more vivid. We find for the first time a peculiar greenish blue, a sort of turquoise, and sometimes a bright royal blue. Some of these figures, such as "The Soldier's Farewell" (220), were listed and illustrated in the

144

221. Uncle Tom and Eva. *c*.1852. 7½ in. 8 in.

222. Archbishop Cranmer. *c*.1851. 9 in.

223. Prince of Wales. *c*.1860. 12 in.

224. Prince Alfred. *c*.1860. 12 in.

225. Huntsman. *c*.1880. 8 in.

(All figures on this page are from the Parr-Kent group.)

145

Kent catalogues (now out of print) right up to 1962. This third category of quality Parr-Kent figure I therefore tend to ascribe to the earliest period of the Kent factory.

For too long the firm of William Kent has been unjustly denigrated by collectors and dealers alike. These earlier products of the factory attained a very high standard and deserve to be judged on their merits. It is true that some of their later figures were not of the same high quality but this is no reason to condemn them all. These late Kent figures should cause the collector no real trouble. The fine combed bases of Thomas Parr, John Parr and early Kent gave way to an ugly blotched base painted in mixed crude dabs of chocolate brown and emerald green. The details of the potting and decoration are in every way inferior and the glaze is poor, thin and dry looking. Even so some modern Kent figures proved exceptions and attained a higher standard. The modern Kent list included not only figures from the Parr-Kent range, but reproductions of much earlier figures from other potters, such as "The Vicar and Moses", "Parson and Clerk" and many others. They can still be found all over England in junk shops, street antique markets and, I regret to say, in many otherwise respectable antique shops whose owners should know better than to offer them as anything but late Kent reproductions. These figures were made with no intent to represent them as being anything but what they were, modern products of a firm with a fine tradition. That is why they look so different from the early Kent figures. Nevertheless they have confused the most surprising people.

Some time ago I took part in the B.B.C. programme about antiques called 'Going for a Song'. If a challenger obtains the highest score for three consecutive programmes the B.B.C. gives a small antique as a modest prize. As I write the programme is still running and I think it one of the best to be seen on television (with a natural like Arthur Negus how could it miss?). I don't often get a chance to mix my two professions and I thoroughly enjoyed taking part. I would have enjoyed it even more if my prize had not been a modern Staffordshire figure made by Kent about 1960. The point of this story is not to put the B.B.C. in a bad light – it was most thoughtful of them to take the trouble to find me something they believed would give me pleasure. It does, however, illustrate the danger of buying without knowledge. I've often wondered what they gave for it.

The Kent factory stopped making reproductions in 1962 and now concentrates on making pottery for industrial purposes. Some of their moulds however are still being used and figures produced from them in another Staffordshire factory, under the direction of Mr Kent (see pages 141, 143). The moulds are now being converted from the original press moulds to the more simply operated cast or slip moulds. Pressing is a highly skilled job but a cast mould can be worked by comparatively unskilled operators. It is almost certainly true to say that, without exception, all

226. Made by Sampson Smith. *c.*1860. $15\frac{1}{2}$ in.

modern reproductions of Staffordshire figures are made by this method. Such figures are usually considerably lighter than the originals, and have much larger holes in the base. Apart from their lightness it is by their colours that they are most easily identified. These particular Kent mould figures are of a high standard but the palette is quite unlike that of the originals, displaying shades of green, puce, and yellow not found in the Victorian figures.

This question of palette is most difficult to explain in any book. No colour reproduction, however good, is accurate enough to convey the fine shades of difference between the originals and the reproductions. To attempt to help collectors in this uncertain way would, I am convinced, prove more confusing than useful. There is no substitute for holding a figure in your hand and receiving guidance from an expert, either a knowledgeable collector or a specialist dealer.

Sampson Smith was born in 1813. His active working life as a potter was from

147

227. Wellington and Napoleon made by Sampson Smith. This is the only original pair known to exist. *c.*1870. 16¾ in. 16¼ in.

about 1846 until his death in 1878, and he is generally thought to have produced vast numbers of our Victorian figures including many of the later flat-back variety. The firm's successors continued under his name after his death until 1963. In 1948 the firm discovered some of the original press moulds in a first-class state of preservation and some reproductions were made from them. As with Kent, the figures were made solely as an exercise in reproducing some of the firm's nineteenth-century figures and, like the late Kent figures, were quite unlike the originals in their colours. After the firm closed in 1963 some of these moulds passed to Lancaster and Sandlands who also for a short time made figures from them. Once again they look exactly what they are, modern reproductions of excellent quality, but missing the weight, colour and glaze of the originals. Like all reproductions of Victorian figures

148

Begging Sailor and Child. *c.*1857. 15½ in.   Colour Plate 8.

they lack something which only age can give, a subtle indefinable quality some-times called 'patina'. Even if the modern potter could use exactly the same clay, colours and glaze (which he can't) the result would still not look right. Nothing can replace the effects caused by a century or more of simple handling – nothing; although it doesn't stop people trying.

As the number of collectors grows, so does the demand, and it was only to be expected that other small factories in Staffordshire would start making reproduc-tions of nineteenth-century figures to meet it. For the most part the ones I have seen are content to make copies of the old favourites, the spaniel dogs, cottages, and the ever-popular hens on baskets etc. They are crazed and stained to appear as near to the originals as possible. There is nothing illegal in this, but collectors should note that it is a common practice when figures are reproduced. The real trouble begins, as we shall see, when rare figures are specifically chosen for repro-duction.

So much for honest reproductions. I will only add that it would make life very much simpler for the new collector, and the inexperienced dealer, if such figures were always plainly stamped on the base with a modern factory mark. Very occas-ionally one finds such a modern mark but the vast majority are unmarked.

Forgeries

A forgery is a figure made with the express purpose of deceiving the ultimate purchaser. I say ultimate for people who make them always take refuge in the statement that they are making honest reproductions and that traders who buy them, buy them as such. I have no doubt that this is so, but it only makes the trader as dishonest as the forger. Sooner or later some of these figures are presented for sale to the public as genuine, and their spurious age, so carefully fabricated by the original manufacturer, lends aid to the deception.

It sometimes happens that an actor is required to play a part wearing very old clothes – let's say a well-worn raincoat. For various reasons it may be that a genuinely old raincoat is not available and so a new one has to be 'broken down' to give an illusion of age. This is far more difficult than you would imagine. You can screw it up, stamp on it, soak it in dirty water and spray it with oil, and it remains obstinately what it is – a new raincoat trying to look old. It may succeed in appearing old to the distant audience, but not at close quarters. Age comes slowly, with hundreds of minute changes, nothing can imitate it successfully, the delicate erosion of time cannot be telescoped. Forgers try very hard, but to the practised eye their efforts are a failure.

Many collectors believe, quite wrongly, that the crazing or crackle often seen in the glaze of some original figures is a certain guide to age. Unfortunately nothing is now easier to reproduce. Special glazes have been invented which craze instantly.

They still don't look 'right' to an expert, but they can mislead a beginner. It should also be remembered that some original figures with a well-fired glaze have not developed this crazing. Crazing is therefore a most unreliable guide for the new collector. There is, however, one type of reproduction crazing which is distinctive enough to serve as a warning.

For some years now a certain group of reproduction Staffordshire figures has been appearing on the market. Not only are the figures themselves reproduced, but so are the simulated effects of age. The crazing is fine-meshed and coffee coloured, an effect probably attained by staining with iron oxide or brown shoe polish. Only rarely is original crazing found as dark as this and then it is not so finely and evenly meshed but is more open and uneven. These figures are not from original moulds, but from new moulds made from a genuine figure; there is consequently some loss of sharp detail. Most of those I have seen are much lighter in weight than the genuine figures but this could easily be overcome by allowing the liquid slip to remain longer in the cast mould, so forming a thicker shell of clay. There is some evidence that this is being done already, for I have seen some falsely aged figures which are much heavier. They are always slightly smaller than the original figures (from which the new moulds have been made); but this is an unreliable guide, as the original figures themselves varied considerably.

The colour palette comes quite near that of the originals, and in addition to the enamel range, both underglaze cobalt blue and underglaze black are used. Some-times the cobalt is very good but I have also seen it looking a bit dull and smoky. The gold used is an attempt to imitate the soft original gold but it does not succeed. To a practised eye it is quite lifeless and when used for titles the cursive script is thin, crabbed, shaky, and mean looking, quite unlike the free, broad, generous, flowing copperplate of the original, which takes up a large area of the base (163 and 70). Both "Stanfield Hall" and "Grace Darling" have been made in this manner. The glaze on these figures is very poor, looking more like a tacky discoloured varnish than a true clear lead glaze. The vent holes are made small and irregular, like the originals; in fact every possible effort has been made to make these repro-ductions appear genuine original figures which bear the signs and patina of age.

So dedicated to his 'hobby' is one gentleman who makes these figures that he spares no effort to improve his technique: the tacky varnish-like glaze and stained crazing is less crude in his latest productions. I took the trouble some time ago to write and ask him for a list of his current range of figures and prices. I can only think that perhaps he was too busy to commit anything to paper in spite of the enclosed stamped addressed envelope. Anyway a list of his figures would be useless to collectors for, within certain economic limitations, he can change it as he chooses. The obvious candidates are those figures requiring reasonably simple moulds but which are yet tempting and attractive to an unwary collector. I have already mentioned "Grace Darling" and "Stanfield Hall" and to these may be added

228. Staffordshire c.1971. No original of this named figure exists. 8¼ in.

229. Staffordshire c.1971. 7½ in.

230. A trap for the inexperienced collector. c.1860. 9½ in. c.1971. 8¾ in.

"Dick Turpin", "Tom King", "Uncle Tom and Eva", "Garrick as Richard III" in his tent and recently the boxers "Heenan and Sayers". I illustrate here a genuine figure of "Heenan and Sayers" (on the left) together with the modern reproduction. There is a marked difference in size, the reproduction being smaller (230).

	Genuine	Reproduction
Height	$9\frac{1}{2}$ ins	$8\frac{3}{4}$ ins.
Breadth	6 ins	$5\frac{3}{8}$ ins

These further differences may be noted. The original has a true clear lead glaze all over and slight crazing. The reproduction has a poor, dull, sticky-looking glaze which does not cover the base rim. The crazing is much more extensive and has been artificially stained. The full stop between Heenan and Sayers is missing and the vent hole in the base is blocked up.

Quite a clever piece of 'double bluff' on some forgeries is the occasional use of bright liquid gold suitably rubbed to simulate the effect of age. Even a knowledgable collector might be forgiven for thinking, 'Well it's not all *that* old, after all liquid gold could have been used as early as 1860 and if it were a modern forgery it would surely have had horrid dull gold, not this bright liquid.' I must also record that the quality of the gold on the "Heenan and Sayers" group of boxers is unlike the earlier poor dull gold of "Grace Darling" and also unlike liquid gold. It is in fact very good.

It may be true that these figures are made and sold in the first instance as honest reproductions. What is quite certain is that by the time they are offered for sale to the public, they have often become forgeries. I am told on very good authority that most of them are exported to America, and I know that reproductions from other factories have also been sent there in large numbers. Small wonder then that some Americans complain about the prices of genuine figures in England explaining that they can buy 'Staffordshire Figurines' more cheaply at home. I'm sure they can, for on my last visit to New York at least ninety per cent of the Staffordshire figures I saw offered for sale were modern reproductions.

This situation is now happily changing as more and more American collectors are beginning to love and appreciate the genuine figures and to distinguish between them and the spurious. There are some very fine private collections in America built up with patience and care through the years. All these collectors were clever enough to seek expert advice in England and their figures now are worth a great deal more than they paid for them. American dealers too are now beginning to buy good pieces to supply a growing demand, and this will undoubtedly increase prices as competition gets fiercer. On the whole it is true to say that England has been quicker than America to see Victorian Staffordshire as an under-estimated primitive art-form well worth collecting, and by far the greatest number of really superb collections are in this country.

152

Fakes

A fake I take to be a genuine figure which has been cleverly altered or doctored in such a manner as to convince a collector that it is extremely rare, if not unique. In practice they are so few and far between that the beginner need not have the slightest qualms about encountering them. They are of mainly academic interest, like the figure which came up for sale at Christie's in January 1969. It appeared in a large sale of English pottery and was catalogued as

> A Staffordshire pottery figure of a Whaler, modelled as a peg legged man standing beside a pillar playing a concertina, in a yellow cloth cap, blue cloak and yellow breeches. Named in capitals on the green base. $7\frac{1}{2}$ inches high.

And very splendid it looked at first sight; most interesting. A closer inspection caused me to note in my catalogue, 'A fake, completely built up and resprayed'. In fact the peg leg, the concertina, and other features were a complete fabrication, later additions to a genuine broken figure, probably of William Shakespeare. It may well have been made up by some restorer with his tongue in his cheek just to see how far it would get. I don't know, but it's a good example of a fake. It was in fact bought by an extremely knowledgeable dealer who hadn't been able to view it before the sale, but realized that if the catalogue description were accurate it must be very rare if not unique. Needless to say it went crashing back to Christie's at such a speed that the reverberations took some time to die down. Had it been bought by a private collector, however, instead of one of our leading experts, it might well still be treasured as a great rarity. Inexpert buying in even the most respectable sale rooms is not without its dangers for the unwary.

Restorations

A restored figure is one which has been damaged and repaired. Restorations worry some new collectors much more than is necessary. Obviously a figure which is in absolutely mint condition is to be preferred to one which has been damaged and restored, but the difference in value is not as great as most people think. Many of our figures are now well over a hundred years old, and pottery, especially pottery which has not been highly prized until recently, has often suffered some minor damage. A hand or a head might well have been knocked off, and stuck back with ordinary glue. An expert restorer can soak off this old brown glue and replace the hand or head so that without specialized knowledge it is impossible to see what has been done. To my mind this is infinitely better than the glue and has never stopped me buying a figure I liked and wanted, which is just as well, for some of them I have never had the chance to buy again. In any case a good dealer will always tell a collector exactly what he believes has been done, and the price will reflect that knowledge; it will depend entirely upon the extent of the restoration and how well it has been done.

Some collectors have great faith in ultra-violet lamps to detect restoration which is supposed to show up very clearly in this light. Perhaps the fault lies with me and not with the lamps but I have never been able to get satisfactory results with them and like many specialist dealers I prefer to use my eyes and sense of touch. A figure which rattles when shaken may have been restored, even though this is not obvious at first. The rattle may be caused by a small chip of loose pottery trapped inside the repaired figure. But this is by no means certain; sometimes, when the potter gouged out the vent hole in the leather-hard figure before firing, the small piece of clay fell inside the figure causing it to rattle in exactly the same way. It should not be forgotten either that vent holes and spill vases could be a great temptation for children. Pins, needles and many other strange objects have been pushed into figures in this way.

Bad restoration is certainly something to be avoided, and I don't just mean those efforts of well-intentioned amateurs who have experimented disastrously with decorators' filling paste or plaster-of-Paris. No figure is improved by guesswork and unless a restorer is working accurately from an identical figure or from clear photographs the work is best left until such time as they are available. Restoration should mean just that – to return as closely as possible to the original. Imagination should have no place in this work.

New collectors, I believe, become unnecessarily obsessed with the search for absolutely mint figures to the exclusion of all others. All antiques go through this phase when they first become popular. A young lover cannot accept flaws in his beloved, an old husband has learned to love with tolerance – even the blemishes. They are, after all, the honourable scars of over a century's fight for survival. Not so many years ago, new collectors felt the same about eighteenth-century Staffordshire, and many now bitterly regret the marvellous opportunities they missed when they look back. A collector should develop a sense of proportion and priority in assessing the merits of a figure. It is sad sometimes to see superbly potted, rare or unusual figures rejected for some minor repair, while mediocre mint figures of infinitely inferior quality are accepted in their place. I don't doubt that some people would refuse to consider buying the Venus de Milo.

To sum up. Fakes, Forgeries, Reproductions and Restorations need not present a great hazard to a new collector. His safest, surest protection is a specialist dealer who will guide and teach him, however modest his first purchases may be, until he is able to be sure of his own judgement. Look at it this way. Quite apart from the pleasure a collection can give, there is no doubt that it represents a personal investment of money, sometimes a considerable sum. Now suppose you were investing in stocks and shares. Is it likely that you would take the advice of someone of whose judgement you knew nothing, and buy shares in a company about which you were equally ignorant? No, of course not. You would, if you were sensible, seek the specialist advice of your bank manager or a reputable stockbroker, and you would continue to follow their advice until such time as you felt able to rely more securely upon your own judgement.

I am not suggesting that only specialist dealers sell genuine figures – that is nonsense. Antique shops all over the country sell them, and there are still bargains to be found, although, inevitably, not so many as there were. That is half the fun of collecting, the excitement of bargain-hunting and the anticipation of what may be tucked away in the back of the shop. But at least be sure of your judgement first. You don't need to buy many reproductions to make the rest of your figures very expensive when you come to add up what you have invested.

As the study and appreciation of Victorian Staffordshire figures has been largely ignored for so many years, it is not surprising that there are very few specialist dealers but for the new collector they are worth seeking out. At the moment the world of the Staffordshire collector is a small one and a reliable dealer is not difficult to find. Talk to other collectors; word-of-mouth recommendation is always the most reliable guide, and advertisements in antique magazines can be judged by the experience of others. With a few exceptions the majority of specialist dealers are to be found in London, but with the rapid growth of interest I have no doubt that reputable dealers in the provinces will begin to devote more time to the detailed study of this most neglected field and will then be able to help new collectors everywhere.

9
Where they were Sold

The marketing of these figures has always been a bit of a mystery, and until now it seems to have attracted little research.

In the late eighteenth and early nineteenth century hawkers collected goods direct from the pottery yard (1) and travelled with them from village to village carrying them in baskets on foot or by donkey or packhorse, for the roads in the Potteries were impassable by cart until the second half of the nineteenth century. These goods appear to have been mostly domestic crockery but it is possible that this method was continued later and used to sell figures. Concrete evidence is hard to find and much remains a matter of speculation. Certainly this would have been a difficult way to have marketed some of the larger, heavier figures. Common sense suggests that these would have travelled by canal and sea and sold in china shops, which were springing up all over the country in increasing numbers.

At the census of 1851 the number of persons engaged in the manufacture of earthenware was listed as 36,512, and the number of persons listed as dealers was 5,728, both high figures compared with other trades. China warehouses are listed in trade directories in London throughout the century, and many of the better-quality figures must have been sold to retailers from them, to find their way to china shops where the demand was greatest.

Some warehouses specialized in supplying crockery and figures to itinerant traders who travelled with goods and families in covered carts or vans. Such 'handsellers' found their way to the remotest hamlets and even to isolated farm-

231. Packing China and Earthenware in "Crates".

houses, where they were sometimes happy to exchange their wares for food instead of money. Some rare figures have come to light when, years later, the contents of such farm-houses were sold at auction. Even today some farm labourer's cottage might well have a small fortune sitting on a mantel-shelf or packed away in a forgotten corner.

Although most of his time was spent prospecting quiet country villages where the china shops of the town couldn't sell, the handseller, in the fine weather of the 'tenting season', was more often to be found in one of the travelling fairs, where for a change the crowds would come to him. 'Chaney ornaments' were specifically mentioned in an eye-witness account of the sheep-and-cattle fair near Bath in 1838. But the trade must have been well established much earlier than this and it continued throughout the century.

The railways were opening up the sea-coast towns as holiday resorts and it seems likely that then, as now, there could have been a steady trade in cheap, gaily coloured pottery to take home as presents. The days when such pottery was actually labelled 'A present from Brighton', or wherever it was, were to come later, although Pugh records seven earlier examples. I suspect that in the 1840s and '50s many of our figures were sold in this way.

Figures of stage stars and personalities would sell best in the towns which boasted a theatre where they appeared. I think, however, that one reason why so many of these recently identified figures were untitled was economic. *The Pilot*, a most successful and popular naval melodrama adapted by Fitzball and others from the novel of Fenimore Cooper, remained in the touring repertory for years and Jerrold's *Black Eyed Susan* even longer. Now there is no doubt that both these figures (9 and 116) are portraits of T. P. Cooke taken from prints, but Cooke couldn't appear everywhere and many other actors played these parts all over England. Not much point, then, in offering for sale a titled figure of Cooke when the part was being played by someone else. It is significant too that the moments from the action of the play chosen by the potters were nearly always the most dramatic ones to catch the eye. The play, and the moment, often sold the figures more effectively than the star; either in the local china shops or from hawker's stalls near the theatre, perhaps both. This was almost certainly the case in London. In the rare 1861 edition of Mayhew's *London Labour and the London Poor*, he says:

In wandering along Whitechapel we see ranges of stalls on both sides of the street, extending from the neighbourhood of the Minories to Whitechapel Church. Various kinds of merchandise are exposed for sale. There are stalls for fruit, vegetables and oysters. There are also stalls where fancy goods are exposed for sale – combs, brushes, chimney ornaments, children's toys and common jewellery.

232. Sir Walter Scott and his favourite hound, Maida. *c.*1850. 14¾ in.

233. Shakespeare. *c.*1848. 9¼ in.

234. A very rare titled bust of Lord Byron. *c.*1845. 8½ in.

Mayhew further records 'stalls selling china, looking glasses, combs and chimney ornaments' in the Mile End Road, the New North Road and 'occasionally in other streets and different localities of London'. It would be very strange if some of the theatrical figures were not offered for sale on stalls outside or near the theatres and places of entertainment where the heroes were appearing in the flesh.

The atmosphere in the crowded street markets was almost exactly like that of the fairgrounds. Mayhew's team interviewed a man who had travelled the fairgrounds with a 'Cheap John', selling cutlery, books, stationery and hardware. When he left to try his luck in London he says: 'I remember on coming to this great city I was much astonished by its wonders and every street appeared to me like a fair.'

At one time I believed I had found definite proof that Staffordshire figures and busts were hawked round the streets of London by so-called 'Italian Image Makers'. There is a music cover showing one of them selling what could be Staffordshire busts from a flat tray on his head. The song was written and sung by Mr Hudson and was called 'Buy my Images'. It included references to Byron, Scott, Shakespeare, Burns, Milton, Nelson and Wellington as well as the Queen and Albert. In December 1815 J. T. Smith published two drawings of these Image Makers, one selling from a tray and another selling from a trestle in the street.

Unfortunately I have since discovered that the images and busts sold by these Italians were made of cheap, fragile plaster-of-Paris, not Staffordshire pottery. Most of them lived in or near Leather Lane and manufactured the plaster figures there themselves. It is just possible that they also sold Staffordshire figures but I doubt it. Every contemporary account of them specifically mentions plaster images,

159

235. Rare Astley equestrian pair said to be Andrew Ducrow and Louisa Woolford. *c.*1850. 10 in.

236. Mr West jun. as Mazeppa at Astley's. *c.*1848. 9⅛ in.

237. Mazeppa on a zebra. *c.*1855. 14 in. In the collection of Surgeon Captain P. D. G. Pugh.

238. Behind the Scenes at Astley's. *Cassell's Illustrated Family Paper*, 5 April 1856.

and never pottery or Staffordshire. It is significant too that they were almost always referred to as Image *Makers*.

The Italians were active about the middle of the century but 'images' were certainly being sold in Vauxhall Gardens in 1826 and probably both earlier and later. These were more likely to be Staffordshire figures, for Vauxhall presented concerts, opera and theatre, including their version of 'The Battle of Waterloo'. The Gardens were extremely popular and crowded, and were not closed until 1859. 'Image Men' sold Staffordshire figures in the streets of London as well as in Vauxhall Gardens but these should not be confused with the Italian 'Image Makers'.

I have already indicated the influence of Astley's productions on the potters. The full extent of this influence is far greater than has been realized. Many of Astley's heroes and villains in the nineteenth century were potted in Staffordshire, and the reason they were potted was because Astley's created a constant demand for them in London and all over England. At one time there were as many as nineteen different amphitheatres where these hippodramas were played before enthusiastic audiences. Many so-far-unidentified equestrian figures must have been inspired by these productions and much work remains to be done on them. Shakespeare, Scott and Byron were all grist to Astley's mill; even opera didn't daunt them and both *Il Trovatore* and *La Sonnambula* were sung in full and partly on horseback in 1857. Dick Turpin and Tom King, Mazeppa and John Gilpin, as well as countless

161

239. Royal Arms. *c.*1862. 9½ in.

Napoleons and pseudo-oriental horsemen, all owe their existence as figures to Astley's. Certainly some figures of Garibaldi were taken from music covers and *The Illustrated London News*, and would have sold well because of his visit here in 1864. But before he ever set foot in England he was a famous figure and the hero of several plays, including an Astley's production in 1859, Tom Taylor's *Garibaldi*. Some of the equestrian figures of him and of 'Garibaldi's Englishman', Colonel Peard, were possibly made for this production before his visit.

Many of the figures of acrobatic horsemanship must be portraits of one of Astley's greatest stars, and one-time manager, Andrew Ducrow. He and his wife were immensely popular and the figures could have represented both them and their countless imitators. The potters followed their market very closely. There is a record of *Mazeppa* being performed at Nottingham with the youth lashed to a zebra instead of the traditional wild horse of Tartary. This version may well have been played at other towns at different times for the potters produced a figure incorporating a zebra (237).

Half theatre and half circus as it was, animals were always a feature of Astley's and similar productions, and it would be easier to name the animals which did not appear there rather than list the many that did. Some of the fox- and stag-hunting figures might well have been made with Astley's audience in mind, for mock versions of both were given in the arena and Ducrow himself once appeared as 'The

162

240. Show woman. *c.*1840.
$7\frac{3}{4}$ in.

Yorkshire Fox Hunter'. There is an interesting aquatint showing the exterior of Astley's as it appeared in 1823. On either side of the pillared entrance can be seen shops; I have no proof, but I can think of no better position for the sale of Staffordshire figures based on the wonders within. A collection of such figures today could be interesting, satisfying, and relatively inexpensive.

Fairs and markets also had a very great influence on the potters. They provided not only inspiration for suitable subjects but a good place to sell them, with crowds of people in a holiday mood to spend money. Fairs have been with us for centuries, certainly since the Norman Conquest and probably long before. Originally the emphasis was on the sale of goods, cloth, pewter, pottery, and of course cattle, horses and sheep. For at least two centuries before the Conquest, itinerant 'professors of the art of amusing' were tramping from town to town and village to village. 'Dancers, posturers, jugglers, tumblers and trainers of animals' found the fairs an ideal focal point with a ready-made audience. Gradually these entertainers became more and more sophisticated and organized, until by the nineteenth century they had become as big an attraction as the market itself. Individual animal acts had developed into menageries and circuses and strolling players now performed in board-and-canvas theatres.

Richardson's was the most famous of these travelling theatres. Well organized, with a large company and a band of ten musicians dressed in scarlet like Yeomen

163

241. Jules Perrot in *Giselle* and Carlotta Grisi. *c.*1842 and later. 9 in. 9½ in.

242. Fairground performer. *c.*1860. 14½ in.

of the Guard, it dominated the big fairs all through the time when our figures were made. It could seat at least a thousand and boasted an elevated stage with a green curtain surmounted by the Royal Arms, with an orchestra lined with crimson cloth. The exterior appears in contemporary prints and made a splendid sight. Formed by a thirty-foot parade wagon, it was backed by green baize and festooned with deeply fringed crimson curtains. The money-takers, wearing jewelled turbans with feathers, sat in elaborate gothic box-offices to accept the sixpence or shilling entrance fee.

To attract an audience show-women bashed tambourines (240) and short free entertainments, often of a very high quality, were performed on these 'parades'. Richardson presented some ballet from *La Esmeralda* on his parade, with new costumes and a new production. A burlesque of the opera with ballet was playing to big audiences at the Adelphi at the time. The potters produced portraits of Carlotta Grisi and Jules Perrot in both *La Esmeralda* and *Giselle* based on music covers, but these untitled figures would also have found a ready sale in the fairground as representing Richardson's now forgotten dancers. This might explain why these particular figures are relatively common and why so many of them were made. Another very popular free show on the parades was a dance of reapers and gleaners and I believe that many figures were based on this and similar entertainments.

Richardson managed to present a new play every day of the fair and the

164

243. Figures in an
unidentified melodrama,
listed in *The Connoisseur* for
1911 as John Philip Kemble
and Fanny Kemble. *c.*1840.
$7\frac{1}{2}$ in.

following is a representative sample. He first presented 'an entirely new melodrama' called *The Wandering Outlaw or The Hour of Retribution* with a cast of seven,
not to mention sundry 'nuns and ladies'. This was followed by a pantomime,
Harlequin Faustus or The Devil will have his Own with a cast of nine not including
'Daemons, Sprites, Fairies, Ballad Singers and Flower Girls'. Not bad for sixpence;
mind you, they got you out in twenty minutes flat, and sooner if an audience was
waiting. The secret cue was a bellowed enquiry in the theatre, 'Is John Orderly
here?' The rest of that performance was given at about the same speed as a
present-day second house Saturday performance in the West End, when some of
the cast want to catch their last train to Brighton.

Many of these fairground melodramas were greatly shortened versions of popular
well-loved favourites. Frost in his book on fairs and showmen says that Selby's
Mysterious Stranger was played in fifteen minutes, 'which thus contracted, became
more mysterious than ever'. Many more were a series of set dramatic situations
probably never committed to paper. Actors knew the story and invented their own
dialogue, fitting in a favourite 'revenge speech' or anything they were fond of
speaking. When I first came to London I worked with an old actor who as a boy
had travelled the fairgrounds playing in such melodramas. Figures in histrionic
attitudes (243) may well have been based on a print, but could have been sold in a
fair as one of a hundred costume heroes or villains.

Fairgrounds were a microcosm of the nineteenth-century world of entertainment.

165

244. The Elephant of Siam at Wombwell's Menagerie. *c.*1840 and later. 6½ in.

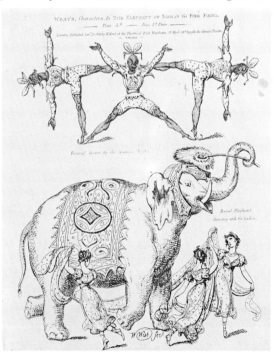

245. 'The Elephant of Siam dancing with the royal ladies'. Toy Theatre print. By courtesy of the Victoria and Albert Museum.

166

Not only theatre, but circus and menageries must have inspired hundreds of figures. Animals and equestrian acrobats would have sold as well in the fairgrounds as they did at Astley's.

The evidence supporting the sale of our figures in the fairs is very strong. Polito's menagerie was the largest and most famous of the travelling animal collections at the turn of the century. Polito died in 1814 and thereafter Wombwell was the biggest. Wombwell himself didn't die until 1850 but the business was carried on by his wife and there were many imitators both large and small. The Zoological Gardens in Regent's Park did not open until 1828 and for the vast majority the fairground menageries were their only chance to gaze on exotic and impossible creatures.

The potter's version of the parade front of Polito's (which later did service for Wombwell's) is very well known and has been illustrated in almost every book on Staffordshire pottery except this one. It shows clearly the performers and musicians in feathered turbans and could never have found a better market than in the fair itself. The same argument applies to the figure of "The Death of the Lion Queen". Being Wombwell's niece, Ellen Bright would only have appeared in fairgrounds where the figure would later have had a ready sale.

The figure of "The Elephant of Siam" (244) puzzled me for some time. There can be no doubt that the dramatic action fits exactly into the plot of the Adelphi Theatre production of 3 December 1829. This 'New and Gorgeous Serio-Comic Indian Burletta Spectacle' was called *The Elephant of Siam or The Fire Fiend*. During the course of the action 'the elephant enters and wrenches the bars from the Princes window'' allowing him to escape by sliding down her trunk and back. This is obviously the moment captured by the potters.

Originally produced in Paris at the Cirque Olympic in 1817, the elephant was imported, together with her trainer, the Chevalier Huguet. The Adelphi succeeded in out-bidding both Drury Lane and Covent Garden to secure her services. Now the trouble is that the Adelphi production is really a bit too early for the style of potting. In any case it was a Christmas entertainment with a very limited run and unlikely to have attracted the commercial instincts of Staffordshire. I reasoned that there must have been a later demand for it, yet there was no evidence of this 'Gifted Female' appearing in any other conventional theatre. A large elephant complete with French trainer is not easy to absorb into society and the obvious place to look for her was the fairgrounds. Sure enough, I found a record of Wombwell securing in 1830 the services of 'The Great Elephant of Siam'. If it is true that elephants never forget I see no reason why she should not have performed this particular rescue trick for many years before Wombwell's audiences, and I have no doubt that the figure was sold in the fairground.

'The Elephant of Siam' had created a sensation at the Adelphi, both for her

167

performance in the play, and for the special solo evening she gave before it opened. This performance when the star, ten feet high and weighing over nine thousand pounds, was put through her paces by Huguet, probably gives a fair idea of her later performances for Wombwell. She balanced objects with her trunk, demonstrated the use of the elephant in war and tiger hunting, accepted money from the audience (which she gave to Huguet), and made 'a grand obeisance'. Warming to the applause, she played 'Elephant Carpenter' and 'Elephant Housemaid', danced and circled the stage on her knees. She lifted huge weights and carried two gentlemen from the audience on her back. Finally she distributed flowers to the ladies in the nearest boxes, drew a cork from a bottle and drank the health of the audience. Few of our leading ladies could do as much today. No wonder she was a great success, no wonder Wombwell bought her, and no wonder the potters saw their chance and slapped her into clay to make a best-seller in the toy shops of the fair. For years this figure has been described, either as "The Elephant of Siam" from the Adelphi production or as "Mr Hemming's Circus Act". Neither is accurate. Mr Hemming was merely the actor who played the rescued Prince and the figure is too late for the play. At one time I thought it possible that Mr Hemming was the elephant's trainer but my latest research has disproved this. The figure is "The Elephant of Siam at Wombwell's Menagerie" and was sold as such in the fairground toy shops.

Frost specifically mentions these toy shops as being bigger than any of the other stalls, some of them having a frontage of over twenty-five feet. The potters themselves referred to their figures as toys and great numbers of them must have been sold in this way all over the country. From about 1860 onwards this vigorous native folk art out of Staffordshire faced foreign competition from Germany in the form of 'fairings'. These must have been considerably cheaper than our figures for vast numbers of them were imported. It is a matter of personal taste, but for me they are beastly little hard paste horrors, like a cheap Victorian novelette where a sniggering kitchen maid has scribbled some minor obscenity in the margin.

It is sometimes difficult to imagine where certain figures would have found a market: Arthur Orton, for example, 'The Tichborne Claimant'. Certainly the case aroused enormous public interest, his supporters believing him to be a baronet, Sir Roger Tichborne, and others being equally convinced that he was the son of a Wapping butcher. I used to think that perhaps the potters made the figure for sale in the streets near the court during the trial. It was indeed the longest trial in British legal history but they could not have anticipated that at the time. I then found that Orton had toured the country in 1872–3 before his trial and after his release in 1884, lecturing to establish his claim and innocence (246). This was a much better commercial proposition for the potters. Most of his fairground audiences were firmly on his side. Melodrama had come to life, wronged innocence must be rewarded and if his claim to the title was rejected by the courts it was granted

246. Music cover by Alfred Concanen. A poster showing the Tichborne Claimant top left and Richardson's Theatre distant right.

247. The Tichborne Claimant. One of the most fascinating mysteries of the nineteenth century. Baronet or butcher? The Press was largely against him but the public and the potters were firmly on his side. This figure shows him in a very favourable light and not as the gross creature he was in 1872 before his trial. It may well have been re-issued in 1884 for he signed a contract to appear in fairgrounds, music halls and circuses on the very day of his release. c.1872. $14\frac{3}{4}$ in.

248. The Fishergirls. c.1851. 15 in.

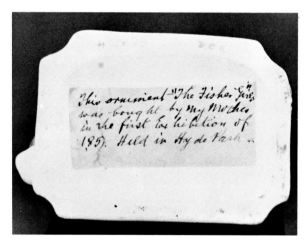

249. Label on base of 248.

250. The shop in Kensington Church Street.

freely by the potters. The figure firmly labelled 'Sir R. Tichborne' in raised capital letters could be included in either a collection of crime or fairground pieces (247).

Apart from fairs, I have recently found some evidence to suggest that at least some Staffordshire figures were sold during the Great Exhibition in Hyde Park in 1851. The figure illustrated here (248) has an interesting old label stuck underneath it: 'This ornament – "The Fisher Girls" was bought by my mother in the first Exhibition of 1851. Held in Hyde Park (249).

All through the nineteenth century travelling fairs brought colour and wonder and gaiety to the remotest corners of the country. For millions Polito, Wombwell, Scowton, Richardson, Sanger and Clarke were names with more magic than Drury Lane and Covent Garden. The Staffordshire figures sold in the fairs caught that colour and wonder and magic and kept it on the mantel-shelves of the people as bright as the music of Wombwell's band. The figures are sold in fairs to this day, but now they are Antique Fairs, and that is a different story.

Select Bibliography

Avery, Gillian. *Victorian People*. London 1970

Balston, Thomas. *Staffordshire Portrait Figures of the Victorian Age*. London 1958

Chesney, Kellow. *The Victorian Underworld*. London 1970

Disher, Maurice Willson. *Greatest Show on Earth*. (Astley's). London 1937

Eaglestone, Arthur A. and Lockett, Terence A. *The Rockingham Pottery*. Rotherham 1964

Frost, Thomas. *The Old Showmen and the London Fairs*. London 1874

Circus Life and Circus Celebrities. London 1875

Godden, Geoffrey A. *British Pottery and Porcelain 1780–1850*. London 1963

Encyclopaedia of British Pottery and Porcelain Marks. London 1964

Haggar, R. G. *Staffordshire Chimney Ornaments*. London 1955

Jewitt, Llewellynn. *Ceramic Art of Great Britain*, (2 Vols). London 1878

Latham, Bryan. *Victorian Staffordshire Portrait Figures for the Small Collector*. London 1953

Mayhew, Henry. *London Labour and the London Poor*. (*4 Vols.*). London 1862

Nicoll, Allardyce. *A History of English Drama 1660–1900*. *Volumes III; IV; V;*. Cambridge. 1963

Owen, Harold. *The Staffordshire Potter*. London 1901

Pugh, P. D. G. *Staffordshire Portrait Figures and Allied Subjects of the Victorian Era*. London 1970

Rahill, Frank. *World of Melodrama*. Pennsylvania State University Press. 1967

Read, Herbert. *Staffordshire Pottery Figures*. London 1929

Rice, D. G. *Rockingham Ornamental Porcelain*. London 1966

Saxon, A. H. *Enter Foot and Horse. History of Hippodrama in England*. Yale University Press. 1968

Shaw, C. (*An Old Potter*) *When I was a Child*. London 1903.

Shaw, Simeon. *History of the Staffordshire Potteries*. Hanley. 1829

The Chemistry used in the Manufacture of Porcelain Glass and Pottery. Hanley 1837

Speaight, George. *Juvenile Drama*. London 1946

Stanley, Louis T. *Collecting Staffordshire Pottery*. London 1963

Trevelyan, G. M. *Illustrated English Social History*. *Volume IV*. London 1963

Wilson, A. E. *Penny Plain Twopence Coloured*. London 1932

Index

Numbers in brackets refer to illustrations.